EPHESIANS:
A Map to Your Incredible Future

by
Maurice
Berquist

Warner Press, Inc.
Anderson, Indiana

All scripture passages, unless otherwise indi-
cated, are from the King James Version ©1972
by Thomas Nelson or the Revised Standard
Version ©1972 by Thomas Nelson.
Copyright ©1989 by Maurice Berquist
ISBN 0-87162-502-4   Stock # D1750
All Rights Reserved
Printed in the United States of America
Warner Press, Inc.
Arlo F. Newell, Editor in Chief
Dan Harman, Book Editor
Cover by Larry Lawson

Dedicated to
Woodrow Starkey who first
inspired me to study
Paul's letter to
the church
at
Ephesus

Table of Contents

Introduction:
Welcome to Ephesians—
Your Map to Treasure

"The greatest week in my life," said Charles Spurgeon, "was the week I read Paul's letter to the Ephesians fifty-six times."

Strange statement. In the light of it, one of two things is true. Either Spurgeon's mind was shallow, or the book of Ephesians is deeper than most of us have imagined.

To my knowledge, no one has dared to suggest that Charles Haddon Spurgeon was a slow learner. While still in his twenties, he pastored the largest congregation in London, England. It grew from five thousand to ten thousand people and became the center of religious activity for scores of other groups. Spurgeon himself was without question the most eloquent voice of his generation—maybe of all generations.

So we are left with the fact that Ephesians may have treasures great enough to tempt even the most casual reader to spend serious time with the book.

Of course the Bible itself is more profound than most of us realize. Ancient scholars have said that "the Bible is an ocean of truth so deep that elephants must swim, but so simple that little lambs may wade in it."

Having said that, I still must say that Paul's letter to the Ephesians is unique. Many, if not all, of Paul's other letters were written to correct some error either of behavior or belief. Ephesians is different. It is a positive statement of the most exhilarating truths that had come to the Apostle's life.

It is both the most otherworldly and the most earthly of Paul's letters. It sees castles in the sky and then builds foundations under them.

In a day when many Christians have neither castles nor foundations, Ephesians promises to be a rewarding study. Does the word "study" seem too threatening? It shouldn't. The Bible itself encourages a person to "study to shew thyself approved unto God, a workman that needeth not to be ashamed, rightly dividing the word of truth" (2 Tim. 2:15). It may be that we lack the brilliance of Charles Spurgeon, who could find exciting secrets in each of his fifty-six readings of this letter, but it is certain that any of us can be challenged to give this amazing letter the opportunity to speak to us. Treasures await those who will.

Ah, treasure. Who does not dream of it? Hapless millions gamble their last dollar in hope of becoming a happy winner.

Acres of Diamonds, the story told by Russel Conwell, is too old to be read by today's youth and so old that it is forgotten by the aged. It tells simply of a man in Africa who sold his farm to start on a search for diamonds. He failed to find any. After a lifetime of searching, he threw himself into the ocean to end his frustrated life. The man to whom he sold his farm picked up a strange-looking rock that glistened in the sunlight. Taking it to a jeweler, he discovered that it was a diamond. His farm was full of them. In fact, the largest diamond mine in the world was on his land. This story keeps repeating itself in today's world.

Frank Garmon and Charlie Farmer, two friends of mine from Florida, like to go diving for lobsters on the southern coast. A year or so ago, they found a spot where the lobsters were plentiful. They marked the place by sighting some buildings on the shore and planned to return the next year.

When they came to the spot (dreaming, of course, of the succulent lobster they would enjoy that evening), they found the area roped off and festooned with signs that said, "Keep Out."

Naturally the men were curious. They asked some sailors on the shore. "Last year we were free to dive and look for lobster here. What happened to change things?"

"Haven't you heard? This area—right where you men were looking for lobster—is the place where a number of Spanish ships were sunk. Millions of dollars worth of gold coins are being taken from these waters."

"Just think," Frank told me, "we were swimming all around that fortune in gold and all we saw were lobsters."

Makes you think, doesn't it?

When I began a serious and intense study of Paul's letter to the church at Ephesus—and, of course, to all of us as well—I felt like apologizing to God. I had looked at a few choice verses and had missed the "secrets" to which Paul kept promising to uncover. The Apostle hinted broadly enough. Words like *mystery, hidden,* and *secret* ought to have stirred my intellectual curiosity if not my spiritual hunger. But I simply let my mind slip into the ruts made by other sleepy intellects. I missed the treasure.

So now I ask you to join me. Let us see what lit the fire that warmed Paul's soul while his body shivered in the damp Roman prison. Let us go back into the waters from which we have taken only a few theological crawdads and find treasures that outshine gold.

Great Is What's-Her-Name

Actually her name was Diana, but who cares? She was also called Artemus, Demeter, and probably a few other names. But great she was. According to legend, a silver image had come directly from heaven to a city on the Mediterranean coast. Whether she was real or not, the image conjured up in their pagan minds was real enough to get them to part with their money, their morals, and their sanity.

"Great is Diana of the Ephesians" became the cry, as the whole world seemed headed for this city on the banks of the beautiful blue sea that washed Asia Minor. A temple—in fact, many temples—was built to house the orgies and celebrations that posed as spiritual worship.

Diana's temple was one of the seven wonders of the world. Four hundred and twenty feet long, one hundred feet high, the roof was supported by one hundred columns. Each of these columns was given by a king, prince, or ruler who tried to outdo all the other royalty in the magnificence of his gift.

Behind the main altar where the silver statue of Diana was kept was the world's largest repository of onyx, gold, and art. Paintings and sculptures crowded the huge area. Again, because people wanted to ingratiate themselves with the goddess, each person tried to outdo the other. In its day, this was the Louvre, the Metropolitan Museum, the British Museum, and Fort Knox all in one.

If we try to understand why people would travel from the ends of the earth to go to Ephesus, we have only to remember that they hoped for some of the wealth to rub off on them. The frenzy of the New York stock market gives us some picture of the intensity of their worship. Shifty-eyed businessmen may have doubted the reality of the stories that were circulated about this voluptuous goddess, but they loved the silver and gold with which her worshipers filled their pockets. Silversmiths outdid each other in their clever icons or idols.

It was hard for me to imagine this splendor as I visited what is left of Ephesus. Fragments of marble columns jutted out from pools of stagnant water. The only music was the croaking of frogs as they resented the presence of an infrequent tourist. I practiced my high school Latin as I look at inscriptions on fallen stones. No one shouted, "Great is Diana of the Ephesians."

It was hard to imagine the sensuality, the nudity, the drunken dances, and the sexual orgies that had made the brazen citizens of Ephesus the wistful, dreamy possessors of depraved minds.

Ephesus is gone. Its only glory is a letter written by a prisoner shivering in his salt-stained robe. Tentmaker, street preacher, poet, and prophet—Paul. He is remembered. He saw past the glitz and glamour to the glory. Amid the stones that were bound to crumble, he saw the church rise triumphant.

The vision never left him. Even when his physical eyes had to look out from rusting prison bars, his inward vision of God's glorious church never dimmed. More importantly, through the inspiration of the Holy Spirit he was able to pull back the curtains of human ignorance to show *us* the vision.

Sometimes the vision is painful. In fact, often it is painful because it shows us how much our human perversity has made us blind.

True, we grow church organizations like mushrooms. And, like mushrooms, they disappear. When carnality carves the fellowship, we moan that the church is dying. The pagan world snickers and says, "Why shouldn't the church die? It was getting old, anyway."

In his letter, Paul assures us that the church has roots that go deep—deeper even than history itself. He knew from his miraculous vision that moral and spiritual drought might make a desert of men's minds.

Pasture in the Flint Hills

My childhood was spend in Kansas, which, for the most part, is as flat as the bottom of a box. In our newspaper, *The Topeka Capital,* was a weekly column called "Peqgy of the Flint Hills." I had no idea where the flint hills were, but I imagined they must have been somewhere in Colorado. It was not until I was grown that I had a chance to drive by the flint hills. They are between Topeka and Wichita, Kansas, along highway 35. As I drove by them, I discovered that they have a gigantic corral there. The flint hills are ranch country.

Ranching in drought-stricken Kansas? I couldn't believe it. And on hills of flint? Impossible. But there is was. Not until I read the book *The Natural Wonders of America* did I discover the reason for this unusual place.

A particular kind of grass flourishes on these flint hills. The roots go down through the tiny crevasses and cracks in the rock to seek moisture. Roots may be as long as fifty-nine feet. Even though the earth may be as dry as last year's bird nest, there is water under the surface. The sun may be blistering, but the grass is nourished from the depths.

This is a parable of the church. Paul, though in prison, was nourished by his roots in the historic faith. We will see this as a theme throughout the book.

If we break our linkage with God's eternal plan, we die. If we maintain connections, we live. Even in the flinty hills of trouble, the Church has flourished. And it will.

Your Path to Personal Power

The theme of the letter is adequacy through relationship. Put plainly, Paul is talking about power. The word explodes like early-morning firecrackers on the Fourth of July. Power—power—power. Here the verses crackle as Paul's pen strikes the parchment in the dreary prison cell. All around are the sounds of earthly power, the clanking of armor, the sound of hobnailed boots hitting the cobblestone streets, the ear-piercing blast of trumpets, the shouting, and the tumult. But Paul is not mentioning these. He never does. He is in tune with a heavenly power that *outlasts, out-performs, outdoes,* and *outranges* all earthly power. Hear his words to the church at Ephesus.

> "Making mention of you in my prayers
> . . . that the eyes of your understanding
> being enlightened; that ye may know
> what is the hope of his calling, and what
> the riches of the glory of his inheritance
> in the saints, and what is the exceeding

greatness of his power to us-ward who believe, according to the working of his *mighty power,* which he wrought in Christ, when he raised him from the dead, and set him at his own right hand in the heavenly places, far above all principality, and power, and might, and dominion, and every name that is named, not only in this world, but also in that which is to come: And hath put all things under his feet, and gave him to be the head over all things to the church, which is his body, the fulness of him that filleth all in all" (1:18-23).

Now this power is localized.

For this cause I bow my knees unto the Father of our Lord Jesus Christ, of whom the whole family in heaven and earth is named, that he would grant you, according to the riches of his glory, to be strengthened with might by his Spirit in the inner man; that Christ may dwell in your hearts by faith; that ye, being rooted and grounded in love, may be able to comprehend with all saints what is the breadth, and length, and depth, and height; and to know the love of Christ, which passeth knowledge, that ye might be filled with all the fulness of God. Now unto him that is able to do exceeding abundantly above all that we ask or think, according to the power that worketh in us, unto him be glory in

the church by Christ Jesus throughout
all ages, world without end. Amen
(3:14-21).

What wistfulness these verses bring! We
dream but cannot do. When all is said and
done, there is more said than done. We plan,
but our plans are neatly Xeroxed for our com-
mittee reports. We study, but we do not per-
ceive. We polish the gun, but we do not pull
the trigger.

One poetic interpretation of this says that we
have all the knowledge we can use; what we
lack is the will to use it. We intend to do things,
but never get to do them. God needs to bless
us with action.

The parable of power is a common one.
When we lived in Anderson, Indiana, we had as
neighbors a delightful family. The father was a
doctor and was able to provide all kinds of toys
for his three sons. At Christmas time, my wife
Berny asked Twila what she could get for her
boys that they didn't already have. "Give them
batteries."

"Batteries?"

"Yes, batteries. All the toys they got last
Christmas aren't running—they need batteries."

Ah, there's the need. Our minds are full of
plans and aspirations, both for ourselves and
our churches. But they need power.

The native hue or resolution is "sicklied o'er
by the yellow cast of thought." Mired in medita-
tion. Fatigued by failure. Stressed out by the
tension between our divine imperatives and our

human imperfections, tired of trying and trying not to be tired, we become pitiful mourners at our own funerals. Like morticians putting pink lightbulbs above the casket to give a lifelike glow to the corpse, we juggle church statistics to prove that we are doing as well as can be expected.

To our weariness comes God's promise of power: power that can not only raise dead plans but dead people; power that can make the world's strongest governments look like a childish fantasy; power that can melt down the glaciers of icy doubt and tumble the towers of Babel.

Where is the power? How do we get it? If there is still power in the blood, how do we get a transfusion?

Paul knew. He based his ministry on it. "My speech and my preaching was not with enticing words of man's wisdom, but in demonstration and in power" (1 Cor. 2:4).

A friend of mine who has struggled to pastor with apparently meager results asked: "How could God have called me to preach without telling me how to do it?"

Have you asked that question?

Paul has the answer. He says that God is able to do "exceeding abundantly above all that we ask or think, according to the power that worketh in us" (3:20). Ah, there it is. We cannot do it with the power we read about, nor the power we envy in someone else's pulpit or practice. It must be the power within us.

Who knows how great that is? A recent

book about the human mind tells us that the brain is so complex that if we could build a computer to do what it can do, it would have to be housed in a building one hundred stories high and as big as the state of Texas. That's huge. It's incomprehensible. But, then, Paul said the love of God was like that.

There are no limits to how far it can go, but there is a limit as to where it must start—it must start within us.

When Ted Bundy, the confessed murderer of at least twenty people, was executed recently, we saw his picture in all the papers and the television screens. He didn't look so bad. He was, in fact, handsome. You wondered how the possibility for so much evil could lurk in the heart of such an ordinary person.

But it was there. "There is a side of me you do not know," he said.

And there is a side of you that you do not know . . . a hidden potential for amazing good. The power is within.

In Anderson, Indiana, my friend Eldon Williams drove me past a large, brick school building. For many years it housed a public school, then Liberty Christian School. Finally it was bought by a couple as a food service factory. Treva (Gressman) May and her husband had expanded their family catering service and it needed more room. But just as they moved in, the Indiana winter struck. Icy blasts and blizzard. Fuel bills skyrocketed. The cost of gas for heat ranged between twelve- and eighteen-hundred dollars a month—an agonizing amount for a small business. Painfully they paid the bills that first winter and hoped that spring would come.

Finally someone suggested that there had been rumors of natural gas in that part of town. A well was drilled—not deep, but deep enough to strike a vein of natural gas. And now they have heat in the winter, cooling in the summer, and cooking fuel all year. It's theirs, absolutely free. They were sitting on top of the answer to their problems.

No wonder Paul cries out that the eyes of our understanding need to be opened so that we can see what is the extent of the inheritance.

We linger too long on our lament. Whatever has been true of the past, it is possible to move into our future with a sense of adequacy—no, more than this—with adequacy itself. Even more—abundant, exceedingly abundant—above all that we ask or think.

The answer is at once simple and complex. It is simple because it is pointed, but it is complex because it involves all of us.

There is no way we can find the power we need without all of us being involved in the process.

Did not Paul say we "may be able to comprehend with all the saints?"

There is much more to be said about God's power: how it can come, what it will do, and how it may be used. But if we are not willing to take the first step to get it, then everything else is simply useless conversation.

3

Paul—
The Extra-Terrestrial
View

At this point I must suggest that you start reading this amazing letter to the Ephesians. Do not, dear friend, say, "I *have* read it."

Most of us have. Spurgeon had read it before he dedicated a week to reading these six chapters fifty-six times. I suggest that you read the six chapters at least three times—each time underlining key words that seem to leap out with astonishing regularity. To get you started, here are a few words to begin noticing: *called, heaven* and *heavenly, mystery, hidden, together, "In Christ."* If you have colored pencils, use a different color for each of these and when you finish reading, flip through the pages. What a kaleidoscope of color will flash before your mind! What a veritable rainbow of promise!

Criss-crossing through this letter glow these same threads, woven together. And it is *together* that they will make a garment of praise, a tent of blessing, and a blanket of security to warm your chilly soul.

Halford E. Luccock wrote a book titled *Marching Off the Map*. He wasn't writing about Paul's letter to the Ephesians, he was simply encouraging people to venture beyond their normal thoughts and behavior patterns. We know Paul did not read Mr. Luccock's book, but we know he obeyed his advice. He was off the map.

Maps record the visions or journeys of those who make them. There are city maps, state maps, national maps, and even world maps. There are even maps of the heavens.

Paul's map is grander than any of these. He reaches not only around the world, but into "heavenly places." He spans not only the dusty dates of all human history, but speaks glibly of what was "before the foundations of the world."

Paul tantalizes us with the prospect of power so great that our own minds cannot map its course. Imagination fails. It is "beyond anything that we are able to ask or think."

Where did Paul get this knowledge? Obviously he got it by *revelation*. And that is how he urges us to get it.

Without question, Paul in his early years was schooled in history. As a boy, he was tutored personally by the highly esteemed Gamaliel. Whatever he had learned as facts of Jewish history was later kindled into a revolutionary flame by the ardor of his own inquisitive and perceptive mind. He became a human coatrack for those who sweatily hurled jagged rocks at

Christian preachers. He became a one-man war against any who could not see that Judaism was God's way of working with people. Any who stood in the way of that vision were promptly put in prison or simply put to death by stoning. Like a hound after a hare, he pursued the early Christians.

But something—in fact several "somethings" —happened to Paul. As the hooves stirred little clouds of dust on the well-traveled way to Damascus, he was hurled to earth by a hand he could not see. He heard a voice from a speaker he could not see. He was blinded to everything around him. He was led away like a prisoner of war. Paul, mighty Paul, who carried letters authorizing him to bring Christians back as slaves, was himself a slave.

In the days of his physical blindness, Paul's mind began to march *off all the maps of religious knowledge.* Who knows what he thought? Whatever it was, it gave him a glimpse of God's plan for humankind. Not merely the "chosen people," but all who willed to be "chosen."

Another experience in Paul's life intrigues us: He was caught up to the third heaven. Read about it.

> I knew a man in Christ above fourteen years ago, (whether in the body, I cannot tell; or whether out of the body, I cannot tell: God knoweth;) such an one was caught up to the third heaven. . . . How that he was caught up into para-

dise, and heard unspeakable words, which it is not lawful for a man to utter (2 Cor. 12:2-4, KJV).

Whatever it was that Paul saw—and he never really tells us—it made him a different man. He could no longer be satisfied with the provincialism of his countrymen. He could not, in fact, be totally satisified with the earth itself. "To be absent from the body," he wrote, "and to be present with the Lord" (2 Cor. 5:8). In Philippians, he says he is "having a desire to depart, and be with Christ; which is far better" (1:23).

Even more important than any personal pleasure that might await Paul in paradise is the view of history he was granted. He was able to look at the plans of God "before the foundations of the world" (Eph. 1:4).

Not only did Paul glimpse the gleam in God's eye as he planned creation, but Paul also glimpsed the *end* of all things—the last day.

Of course, neither Paul nor any person since Paul has any idea of when that last day will come: the Bible clearly tells us that. But Paul did see what would happen when all of God's plans are complete. "That in the dispensation of the fulness of times he might gather together in one all things in Christ, both which are in heaven, and which are on earth; even in him" (Eph. 1:10, KJV).

It seems certain that Paul was in a Roman prison when he wrote to the church at Ephesus. If it is the same one that tourists are shown today, it was a large abandoned well. Water flowed under it, chilling and dampening the mossy walls. Meager rations were let down to the prisoners by a rope. When the prison became too crowded, some unfortunate prisoner was dropped through the well opening into the underground river. Gloomy as this was, it did not depress the apostle. He endured the *present* because he had seen the *future*.

What a balance this brought to his life. "I know both how to be abased," (how well he had learned this) "and I know how to abound" (Phil. 4:12). Neither the grimness of the prison nor the grandeur of palaces impressed him. He had seen visions too spectacular to put into words. No small thing when we consider that Paul was a master of words—words in many languages.

Because of these visions, Paul writes to instruct the Ephesians. His message is clear: Friends, you have an inheritance greater than I can describe to you. But I will pray that God will open your eyes. He will even give you a little glimpse of its magnitude, but don't think you can understand it. Your mind cannot take it in. And I can't find any words that do it justice. It is a source of power—and I am going to tell you how to receive that power. God has great plans for you. Don't miss them.

4

Your Future Is in Your Past

"Have you lived here all your life?" a tourist asked a whiskered old man in front of a village store.

"Not yet," he answered.

Of course he hasn't. But neither have you. In fact, even if you are a sickly, aged, and decrepit shadow of a human being, you have not yet lived all your life—eternity stretches ahead. Death may come, but that is not the end.

Insurance statistics may tell you how long you may expect to live and pay premiums, but no one can tell you how long life will last—no one except the person who gave you life—God.

At the other end of the spectrum, we pat a child on the head and, for want of any better conversational material, say, "And how old are you?"

The answer depends upon the maturity of the child. Younger children tend to give their age—"I'm three." As they older, they tend to express their ambitions, "I'm five, going on six."

Neither of these answers are correct. Mathematically, perhaps, they are satisfactory, but from the viewpoint of Paul, they are not only skimpy, but untrue.

Paul writes "He hath chosen us in him before the foundations of the world" (Eph. 1:4). He has "predestinated us unto the adoption of children."

Predestination is a frightening word to many. It shouldn't be. Breaking it down, we find two principle parts: *pre*—meaning "beginning," and *destination*—meaning "end." It is simply one more alpha-omega in the Scriptures.

Whether or not the word *predestination* frightens us, or, possibly, comforts us more than it should, it is an uncommon word in our conversation and a common practice of our everyday life.

The end is always contained in the beginning. The timid bride, making her first cake *pre*sumes that she can do it. She *pre*pares the eggs, flour, milk, and baking powder. She *pre*sents these strange ingredients to each other and *pre*heats the oven. She then *pre*sides over the baking and awaits the destination—the cake.

When the cake comes out of the oven, she is not surprised when it turns out to be what she had predetermined it would be. Its destiny was set. The end was in the beginning. The alpha in the omega.

She is, in a sense, a god in her kitchen. She is sovereign.

She is a creator.

Every creative act follows that same pattern. An architect is not surprised when a house turns out to be as he pre-planned it. A composer is not surprised when his work turns out to be a song instead of a recipe for cabbage soup.

Since the believers in Ephesus were Gentiles—non-Jewish, that is—they would not have been familiar with the writings of David, the song-evangelist of the Old Testament. Had they been, they would have known about the predestination concept.

> . . . I am fearfully and wonderfully made.
> . . . My substance was not hid from thee, when I was made in secret, and curiously wrought in the lowest parts of the earth. Thine eyes did see my substance, yet being unperfect; and in thy book all my members were written, which in continuance were fashioned, when as yet there was none of them. How precious also are thy thoughts unto me, O God! how great is the sum of them! If I should count them, they are more in number than the sand . . . (Ps. 139:14-18).

Earlier in this book I told you of the observations of modern scientists that the human mind is so powerful that it outshines any computer we can construct. If we indeed could make a computer that could do what the mind can do, it would have to be housed in a building one hundred stories high and as big as the state of Texas.

Can you imagine that? Of course not. It seems infinite. But even Texas is not infinite—it only seems that way. God is. And that is why he can make infinite (endless) plans for you.

Naturally you can't see this. You can't even imagine this. You can't comprehend it even if there were someone clever enough to explain it to you.

No wonder Paul prayed for you that "the God of our Lord Jesus Christ, the Father of glory, may give unto you the spirit of wisdom and revelation in the knowledge of him: The eyes of your understanding being enlightened; that ye may know what is the hope of his calling, and what the riches of the glory of his inheritance in the saints, And what is the exceeding greatness of his power to us-ward who believe" (Eph. 1:17-19).

Two stories, both as true as they are amazing, follow:

My friend, Joe Bryant, told me of an employee whom I shall, for the moment, call Sam. Obviously that is not his name, and when you hear his story, you will know why I give him the protection of a fictitious name.

Sam was a good-hearted, hard worker. He drove a truck for Joe's plumbing business . . . just a good-hearted, hard-working truck driver who delivered merchandise and kept the contractors happy.

But Sam was not your ordinary blue-shirt worker, he had a romantic streak. He liked to put flowers on the desks of the women who worked in the office. As I get the story, the women were embarrassed by this. There is, as you women know, one thing that is worse than not getting flowers from someone you like—it is getting flowers from someone you don't particularly like.

Being snubbed didn't discourage Sam.

One day two well-dressed gentlemen showed up at Joe's warehouse. They asked for Sam. They didn't explain their mission, they simply asked for Sam the truck driver.

When Sam appeared, they asked him his name—first and last. Then they asked his father's name. As soon as they had satisfied themselves that they had indeed found the man they were looking for, the explained their reason for seeking him.

"An uncle of yours died, leaving you some money. As a matter of fact, a substantial amount of money. And since you claim the name and can prove it, you now have six million dollars—tax free."

Sam kept on driving a truck for a while, but his acceptance level around the warehouse changed perceptibly. He quit sending flowers to get a little acceptance. He probably had more acceptance than he could handle from that time forward. He was, to use Paul's Ephesian phrase, "accepted in the beloved" (Eph. 1:6).

This modern story is simply a repetition of what Paul is describing. God is looking for you. A vast inheritance awaits you. You didn't earn it. You didn't even know about it. You don't even have to deserve it. In fact, there is nothing you can do to deserve it.

You can simply open your eyes to the possibility—or more correctly, let God's spirit open your eyes—and claim it. Of course, you have to establish your relationship to the one who "willed" all this for you. Then claim what is yours through God's grace.

Deceptively simple? Yes, of course. It is simple, but deceptively so. Relationship is the secret ingredient and it is the one place where most of us miss the blessing. Living in *relationship* to God and to the rest of God's family are two sides of the same coin. It is not easy. Possible, but not easy.

Not only is relationship the theme of my book, it is the theme of Paul's letter to the Ephesians. All of which leads me to say that the Bible is not a book to be understood and then obeyed; it is a book to be obeyed. Understanding may or may not come.

Recently, a Bible-publishing company wanted to publish a deluxe gift edition of the Scriptures. The directors were discussing the various types of leather that might enhance the appearance and elegance of the book. Should the cover be morrocco leather, eel skin, or some even more exotic leather?

"I suggest we put the Bible into shoe leather," suggested one director.

Paul's letter to the Ephesians is a good place to start putting the scriptures into shoe leather —into our daily walk and practice.

Simply put, if you want to improve (1) your *relationship* with God, simply let God's spirit first of all convict you about (2) your *relationships* with people; then you should correct these relationships and confirm (3) the *relationship* you have with the called family of God, the church.

A vast inheritance, one beyond your power to imagine, not to mention describe, awaits you. Knowing who you are in relation to God's predetermined plan of salvation is the first step in discovering what that plan is, and what your "inheritance in the saints is."

My second story, also true, does not need to conceal the real name of the hero. His name is Leslie.

In Wichita, Kansas, I was invited to a chicken dinner, not an uncommon experience for a visiting preacher.

After a delicious meal, my hostess asked, "Would you like to hear our grandson play the violin?"

Friends, a violin expertly played makes the angels envious. The gateway of hell is serenaded by beginning students. I was not enthusiastic, but I was polite and, frankly, obligated.

"Yes, please," I said, smiling a thin smile.

"Leslie is going to play on a violin his grandfather made."

My smile dimmed. An amateur solo on a homemade violin was not a joyful prospect.

A handsome young man appeared. The instrument he proudly carried justified his pride; it was beautiful. He began to play a hymn, and I found myself entranced with the mellow music. When he finished, he said, "I played that for my grandparents. They love that song. Now I will play one of my favorite pieces."

Not being a musician, I didn't recognize the impressive name of the music he was going to play, but it sounded like something I ought to have known if I were going to make any claim to culture. At any rate, it was magnificent. A difficult piece to play, but worth all the skill and effort it required. When he finished playing it, I was too awed to applaud. Finally I asked.

"How long have you been playing the violin?"

"I started taking lessons when I was five."

"Oh, that explains it," I said.

"Not really. I took lessons when I was five, but I never really learned to play well until last year."

"And last year?" I asked.

"I attend Wichita University and play in the philharmonic orchestra. I played second-chair violin. The first-chair violinist, the concert master, as they are called, was a girl. I envied her position. I wanted to play first-chair violin. I began a study of the concert masters of the world's best-known orchestras and discovered that ninety-five percent of them are Jewish.

"What could I do? I am not Jewish. I am Irish. Then I remembered a verse our pastor had pointed out. It is in Romans. 'For he is not a Jew, which is one outwardly; neither is that circumcision, which is outward in the flesh: But he is a Jew, which is one inwardly; and circumcision is that of the heart, in the spirit, and not in the letter; whose praise is not of men, but of God" (Rom. 2:28-29).

"So," Leslie continued, "if there is anything that makes Jewish people better violinists, I could claim whatever the *inheritance* is. I am the seed of Abraham. I am in the genetic line of all the great musicians, before and after David the psalmist. When I realized that, there was such a change in my playing that my teacher could not resist asking, 'What has happened to you?'

"I am now first chair . . . the concert master."

Hearing this story, I saw an entirely new dimension to the "inheritance of the saints."

Paul apparently grasped this. Again and again he tells his Gentile friends that whatever there was that separated them from the covenant of promise, (see Eph. 2:12) that wall has been broken down by Christ. "He is our peace who hath made us both one" (2:14).

Whatever strengths, abilities, promises, and powers resided in the apostles and prophets, we are building upon them. They are our strengths, our abilities, and our promises. We need to claim them. We need to affirm our relationship.

Is this a mystery?

Paul said it was.

The late Buckminster Fuller observed that this universe of ours is only a safe combination lock that's located on the inside.

Paul said the universe is a secret vault, with the combination "*in Christ*" (Eph. 3:6). Then he says that we are in Christ (see Eph. 3:14-17). Ten times he says, "in Christ" in the letter to the Ephesians.

Christ unlocks the mystery. He reveals the secret. And, if we despair of understanding who Christ is, the Bible promises that the Holy Spirit will "reveal him." The Spirit also will affirm our relationship to Christ.

One more warning: We cannot be "in his person" while we are not "in his people."

That is the theme of the rest of the Book of Ephesians. It is not difficult to relate to God through Christ. The place where we forfeit power is in broken relationships with people.

Restoring relationships must become the responsibility of every Christian.

Togetherness was ever on the mind of E. Stanley Jones. One of his most pithy observations says that the church can't go much further than it is without first going deeper. Then he adds that it can't go deeper until it commits itself to going together.

Jones is right.

5

Power to
the People of God

Is any problem you have more difficult than the Resurrection?

There was, you know, a resurrection. Spears and nails, crosses and thorny crowns guaranteed it. And the most methodical, brutal, inhumane government in the world declared it was so. Then, with an amazing inward fear, they put the body of a teacher who claimed to be God into a tomb carved out of the unyielding rock. A stone door was fixed and, to add a touch of thoroughness verging on the ridiculous, they posted soldiers to watch this drama of a dead man sealed in a tomb of rock.

The body was as dead as the stone shelf on which it lay. The spirit had returned to God. "Into thy hands I commend my spirit," Jesus said (Luke 23:46).

At that moment there was no power in the body. The power was above the body. And it was as Paul says, "Above all principality [Rome included], and power, and might, and dominion, and every name [Caesar included] that is named, not only in this world, but also in that which is to come . . ." (Eph. 1:21).

Nothing can resist power like that. And nothing did.

The stone rolled back, the grave clothes unwound, the sleeping cells of Jesus' body, the cytoplasm, the protoplasm, and the nuclei all felt it.

The coronation of the king of the universe could not be disputed. <u>God raised the body of Jesus from the dead, making a mockery of all earthly power</u>s.

Shame-faced death stood helplessly by while the king of kings rode off in triumph. So great was the power of God that when Christ's spirit was ascending to the Father, the reverberations caused an earthquake, graves were opened, and those who were in them were strangely stirred with life. After the resurrection, they came out of the graves and into the city and were seen by many (Matt. 27:52-53).

Power without limit—infinite. And, amazingly, power that can come to us.

And what is the exceeding greatness of his power *to us-ward* who believe, according to the working of his mighty power, which he wrought in Christ when he raised him from the dead, and set him at his own right hand in heavenly places (Eph. 1:19-20).

The most amazing part of this whole story is the phrase "to us-ward." In looking at history from before time to the time when time will be no more, Paul has seen the purpose of God's power. It is to do for us what he did for Christ. He raised Jesus. He will raise us. He made a mockery of all the combined powers of politics, personality, purse, and persecution. Nothing can withstand that power. It is true that death is still our enemy, unconquered—but it will indeed be destroyed. The last enemy to be destroyed is death. "Death is swallowed up in victory" (1 Cor. 15:54).

Not long ago, I stood at the empty tomb of Christ in Jerusalem. (I know there are two places that claim to be the authentic tomb of Christ. No matter, they are both empty.)

Standing in that empty tomb, I thought, "Someday the tomb in which I shall be buried shall be opened. The dark, damp earth that walled in my decaying body will be flooded with light. The power of the resurrection shall have come."

But I do not wait until then. The other enemies I face until that time must also bow to the power of God. I should not be surprised when miracles happen. I should instead be surprised if they do not happen.

Not long ago, as I attended an international convention, I was stopped by a woman I did not know.

"You are Maurice Berquist," she said.

"Yes."

"I read your book *The Miracle and Power of Blessing* and enjoyed it, so I read it to my brother."

I wanted to ask why she had read it to him instead of letting him read it himself, but I simply listened.

"My brother," she said, "was blind."

"*Was* blind?" I asked, emphasizing the word *was*.

"As I read to him the book about Psalm 103, God suddenly restored his sight. He now has 20-30 vision."

Why am I surprised by this? Why do you find it difficult to believe? This same power that raised Jesus from death is *to us-ward*.

No wonder Paul prayed that our eyes would be opened so that we could see the extent of the power of God at work in our lives, our communities, and our homes.

So much of our worship is a pious repetition of static truth instead of a celebration of the present power of God. If our ideas, our theology, and our doctrines were to suddenly come to life, we would suspect God of unfair invasion. If our theological gingerbread men were suddenly to come to life and run down the street, we would chase them, tie them, and put them back in the worship folders where they belong. Vitality is frightening.

One day I watched a little child sitting on the mechanical horse in front of the supermarket.

The horse was cold and still, innocent of life as a fireplug. The child had an active imagination and was bouncing up and down in the saddle, making believe that the animal was real and that he was the Lone Ranger.

A stranger coming by dropped a quarter in the appropriate slot. The horse started to move, pitching forward and backward. The child, half-frightened and half-pleased, held the reins tightly. "He's alive, he's alive," he cried.

The parking lot parable is needed by the church. When someone pays the price, things begin to happen. Ancient creeds no longer have to be defended or argued. If they were ever true, they are true today. If they were not true, their falsehood becomes obvious. They can be discarded.

Do we need an infusion of that kind of power? What a waste of paper to write such a question! What a waste of energy to read it!

Our weary routines of trying to do God's work with the power of unspiritual people leaves us with burn out, stress, contention, and flimsy explanations.

Oh, we talk about it, but as one observer put it, "When all is said and done, more is said than done."

Good news—the Resurrection power is available. It is promised. And Paul instructs the Ephesians (and us) in the use of it.

6

What Paul Saw that He Couldn't Tell

"I knew a man . . . (whether in the body, I cannot tell; or whether out of the body, I cannot tell)" Paul said, describing his vision in the letter to the Corinthian church (2 Cor. 12:2).

The fact that he didn't have words to describe what he had seen didn't keep him from trying. Like a dog tied with a short rope, he keeps stretching words to the breaking point, although he knows they will short. He had a glimpse of the cosmos—the universe—everything that ever was and ever will be.

He is not the only one who was ever enchanted by such a vision. As far as we know, he is the only one who ever actually saw it. Speculations are as frequent as sunrises. Theories abound. Philosophers develop theories and scientists probe the secrets of the world's beginning. But it is no use. Rarely will a scientist's theories last as long as his life. That is not to say that scientists are stupid, or that they are wrongly motivated. Indeed, I have nothing but admiration for the inquisitive minds that have probed earth's mysteries. It is simply that humans can't get out of themselves to look at themselves. The brain that analyzes the brain is still a brain. Being immersed in the world means that we cannot see the world.

A fish in the ocean doesn't know that he is wet.

But Paul rose above the world, into the "heavenlies." It is doubtless more difficult for us to understand that journey than it was for the people of Paul's day. The devout Jew believed that there were three heavens: (1) the heavens where the birds fly and the clouds are; (2) the heavens where the stars are and, (3) the heavens where God is.

Even in our day, we can understand the difference in vision when we rise to the first heaven. Flying on a plane, we can look down upon whole cities at once, we can see the twisting courses of rivers and we see both sides of town at once. If we were astronauts (which most of us are not), we could see the earth in space, much like the full moon appears to us now. But we cannot rise above the earth and the planets and constellations to see eternity, to see the place where time begins. We can see the evidence of creation, but we cannot see the mind of the creator.

Daring scientists can speculate about the earth's origin, but Paul was able to see what there was before the foundation of the world. He saw what was in the mind of God.

No wonder he ran out of words.

He could simply tell us how he was able to see with spiritual eyes things beyond the realm of the natural. He tells us how we can see some of these same things. But it is not easy. We are bound by time-consciousness.

As I write these words I am a guest in the home of Kreston and Lenora Norholm in Oklahoma. In the living room from which I have just come are eight clocks, all running. While I was in the room, wearing my watch, there were nine timepieces. Not one of these clocks can tell how much time there has been nor how much time there will be. We are locked into time. Paul saw beyond it.

"Before the foundation of the world," he wrote that God had predestinated us (Eph. 1:4). Our end was determined before our beginning.

Today, as in Paul's day, God is calling us to fulfill our destiny. And as Paul assures us in another of his writings, "Faithful is he that calleth you, who also will do it" (1 Thess. 5:24). What God has called you *to be* he can give you the power to *become.*

If you had never seen it happen, could you believe that an oak tree resides in a tiny acorn? An oft repeated proverb says, "Anyone can count the seeds in an apple, but no one can count the apples in a seed."

Are there secrets to discovering this power? Of course there are. Again and again Paul speaks of a mystery, a secret, a secret hidden for the ages, until now. He speaks of revelation (uncovering) and insight.

While in an earlier chapter I spoke disparagingly of the goddess Diana, I have to admit that the idea of such a person might have been highly attractive to me had I lived in Ephesus at that time. The image of Diana was said to have come to the earth—even to Ephesus—from heaven. She was a link with the infinite. Who would not like to be on her good side? Even pagans want to hear from some eternal place.

Are not our papers periodically denying the reality of UFOs (Unidentified Flying Objects)? Whether pointy-headed little men actually come to earth on flying saucers may be open to question, but the desire to see such creatures is certainly beyond question. If there are no messengers from outer space, we certainly seem to wish there were.

At the moment, a wave of "New Age" mentality is filtering into our culture. Turbaned gurus and bejeweled mystics ride in limousines and live in million-dollar houses because common people want to hear about "their former lives" or their beyond-time experiences.

How simple it would be if we would believe God's word! We can go beyond time. We can be linked with the eternal. We can be energized with mystic power, the power of the Spirit. We can be united with not only the mind of the universe, but also the mind behind the universe—God.

Can you want more than this?

Can you trust divine revelation more than human imagination?

Even the most fertile human imagination cannot picture what God has planned for you. "Eye hath not seen, nor ear heard, neither have entered into the heart of man, the things which God hath prepared for them that love him. But God hath revealed them unto us by his spirit" (1 Cor. 2:9).

If you do not listen to the Spirit of God, you will not know what treasures are promised you. For example, blind men in Ali Baba's cave would be as content to carry out a handful of rocks as a handful of rubies.

Small wonder Paul prays for the opening of our eyes!

When our eyes become opened enough to realize that they must see more than we are capable of seeing, we can look only at God's promise.

He is able to do exceedingly, abundantly "above all that we ask or think, according to the power that worketh in us" (Eph. 3:20).

In an earlier book, *The Miracle and Power of Blessing*, I described a law of electrical power that can introduce Paul's concept of power. We state it here simply by drawing some lines.

38

God's Eternal Plan and Power
_____
_____

According to the laws of electricity, when there is power flowing on these lines, it is possible to induce it into another wire without any physical connection. You simply put another wire—not connected to anything in any place—underneath these wires. The moment that it gets in parallel with these overhead wires there is a transfer of power. The inert wire becomes charged with electricity.

God's Eternal Plan and Power
_____
_____

God's power and plan in our
lives
_____

If you can allow your mind to believe that these overhead wires stretch to infinity, you will begin to understand the greatness of the power of which Paul speaks. There is no beginning and there is no ending. Before the world was, God is. When the world is no longer a reality, God is. His plans for you pre-date the world and will survive *after* the world.

Your earthly life, on the other hand, has a definite beginning and a definite end. The lower line in this illustration represents your life. You can put a date on the first end of it, but you do not know when the end of it will come.

The great news, however, is that when your life is lined up with the purpose and power of God, you get an infusion of eternity. You are linked to eternal power.

There are many illustrations of this in the world of simple science. If you happen to live near major power lines, you can take a fluorescent bulb and put it under the wires, even at a considerable distance, and the light will begin to glow. The molecules are activated from above.

Even easier to prove is the spiritual principle. If you do what God does, you get his power to do it. If you forgive people, you are forgiven. If you give to others, God gives to you. If you are merciful, you obtain mercy.

On the other hand, if you are unforgiving, you are unforgiven. If you do not give, you cannot receive from God, if you are not merciful, you are denying yourself mercy.

The physical principle illustrates this. If the secondary wire is out of parallel, crosswise, the field of power is cut and no power is transferred. While Paul certainly was not thinking about electricity when he wrote to the Ephesians, he did understand the principle. Harmony with God's will brings blessing, he taught, and disobedience and disharmony brings death.

Chapter two of Ephesians is a short course in how *not* to succeed in the Christian life. We shall look at it in the next chapter.

The funeral was designed to be more of a frolic than a funeral. But no one was fooled. The body, with one-thousand-dollar bills stuck between the stiff fingers, was dead. Whether or not the hands rested on the floral steering wheel, they were powerless.

Ephesus was like that. So Paul wrote to the people who could remember the days when they were caught up in this dance of death. They are now alive enough to know that what they had been promised by the world was not provided by the world. They had discovered that the worship of Diana the goddess did not make them godly or assure them of heaven.

Lest they forget how they came to be so fooled, Paul goes back and points out the road signs on the dead-end street of the sinful life.

What did they do wrong? Dead people do not need an explanation, they need a resurrection. So Paul begins with that fact. Life, new life, has come or they wouldn't have known that they were dead.

Our problem is different. As was the problem of the church in Ephesus—or should we say those who were not in the church in Ephesus?—dead people do not ask for a resurrection. They only recognize a resurrection after it has occurred.

A story is told of a tramp watching an elaborate funeral of a man who insisted on being buried in a Cadillac automobile. Seated behind the wheel of the car, surrounded by flowers,

Dead End Street:
Back Up and Get Out

Redemption. You *cannot* do it without God
and God *will not* do it without you. Since
God's quickening spirit is all around us, it becomes obvious that we must do something in
response to it.

To the casual tourist, Ephesus, with its flam-
ing torches and glittering silver, seemed like a
lively place, but it was a little like that dead fish
I saw on the beach one moonlit night. The
silver of the fish glistened in the moonlight like
a jeweled trophy. You had only to get close to
it to smell its offensive odor and had only to
kick it with your foot to realize it was dead.
Death is death—no matter how it is camou-
flaged, no matter how deceivingly beautiful.

Recently a magazine article told of a young
man who had died after a short and flamboyant
life. His parents arranged to have a casket
made like a golden Jaguar. There was even a
windshield in front of the seated corpse.

the corpse was being lowered into the grave. The tramp watched, fascinated. Then he spoke: "Now that's what I call living."

We smile. We recognize the sly envy of sleepy Christians. Seeing the glitter of godless living, hearing the laughter of empty hearts, we are led by the Pied Piper of Death to the cemetery of sin.

To change the figure of speech, we move to Ezekiel's graveyard—the valley of dry bones (Ezek. 37). As much as Ezekiel might have wanted to hear an anthem, a testimony, or even a complaint from his calcified congregation, there was no sound. Had there been, it would have been only the rattle of death.

Only the powerful voice of prophecy, the breath of God, could waken the dead bones. Only the power outside themselves could bring life within themselves. Only the movement of the Creator could be creative.

It is the same today.

Where spiritual deadness exists, there is no awareness of it. People are not swarming to church seeking life. They are not aware that they are dead.

I do not mean to say that the people who need resurrection are physically dead. They may, as Paul says, live in pleasure, but they are dead while they are living. Like wooden marionettes, they are pulled by strings to dance the macabre dance of death which they call "Living."

Only after new life comes are they able to see their origin, the place from which they have come. Only then can they look back and see the tire tracks where they skidded off the road. Only then can they see the tombstones that marked the time and place of their demise.

Mark Twain once read his obituary in the newspaper. He commented, "The reports of my death have been greatly exaggerated."

Could it be said that reports of our life in this century have been greatly exaggerated?

Now as Paul writes to the people of Ephesus, doubtless Gentiles who had recently come to Christ, he reminds them of the error of their ways—the errors that brought them death.

Sin by any Other Name

A little girl was asked by her Sunday school teacher, "What is the first thing we must do if we want to be forgiven?"

"We have to sin."

Correct. But that isn't our problem. We have all sinned, says the Scripture; the two questions are how did we get into that condition and how can we avoid it. If we think of sin merely as a long list of things we don't want to do anyway, we are missing not only the truth, but also the chance to be forgiven. Sin, as Paul says, is both wide and deep. It is not a simple thing. It deserves serious thought.

Paul uses two words—*trespass* and *sin. Trespass* is a willing violation of a known law. When the sign says "Keep off the grass" and I walk on it anyway, that is a trespass. We know something is wrong, but we do it anyway.

On the other hand, the most common word for sin in the New Testament means "missing the mark." That seems a little less fearsome. We wanted to do right, but we simply failed. After all, we are human.

Could it be that we fail because we will to do so? We made a choice and the choice was to do something wrong. Then we do indeed fail and become frustrated. We sin, but perhaps it is also a sin of omission. We know what should be done, but the cost of obedience is too great.

On the other hand, sin may appear so glamorous and rewarding that we are tempted to disobedience.

Granted, we as Christians tend to blame our human nature for our sin. That is the way we are—we "fall short of the glory of God," just as Paul said we would (1 Cor. 3:23). But if we are totally honest, we have to realize that most of our failure comes because we deliberately trespass—we go against what we know. The warning may be ever so slight, but it is there. And when we go against it, we miss the mark of the high calling of God in Christ Jesus.

Much of our sin is our "being," but much is also in our behavior. Paul gets to this later in his letter to the Ephesians.

Most errors in personal theology come from imbalance. When we emphasize any side of any issue and ignore the other, we distort the truth. In fact, Paul says that we "change the truth of God into a lie" (Rom. 1:25). In the question of sin, it is easy to emphasize one side of the responsibility and ignore the other. We can say that we do what we do because of what we are, and that is, in a sense, true. Or we can say that we *are what we are* because of what *we do,* and that is also true.

The only true balance is that of Scripture which emphasizes both the grace of God and the obedience of man. Paul will deal with this later in his letter.

Can it be that we have died and no one has bothered to write an obituary?

It is only after we have been energized by the life of Christ that we recognize the seriousness of our condition. When the psalmist talks about the horrible pit from which he was dug, he is already out of it. At the time he didn't know that he was in a pit; perhaps he thought that all the world was miry clay. After all, a fish in the ocean doesn't know that he is wet.

It is no accident that Paul addressed his letter to the *saints* in Ephesus. The other people would not have listened to it. Only those pronounced "holy" by the grace of God respond to his call to pursue holiness. The others don't know that they are unholy and have no ambition to become holy.

In their deadness, they paint the corpse with flesh tones and imagine that this is life.

When a popular entertainer commits suicide, all the couch-potato commentators say, "There was no reason for this . . . he had everything to live for." Everything, that is, but life.

I saw a magazine cover that displayed a well-dressed, beautiful young woman. She was saying, "I have an ocean-front apartment, interesting, well-paid work, my sex life is great, and my roller skates cost one hundred dollars. Why do I feel like I am missing something?"

Why, indeed? She's dead. For a few thousand years, Egyptian mummies have resided in their wooden boxes, looking as lifelike as they did when they sailed on the Nile. But they are dead.

It is doubtful that the inhabitants of a cemetery argue much about which one has the most elaborate tombstone.

In his letter to the Ephesians, Paul lists the causes of death. He conducts a spiritual autopsy, a post-mortem. There are two reasons this is important. First, we can look back and see where we went wrong in the first place, and then we can look to see where other people go wrong so that we can avoid their error. Both reasons are valid.

What is the germ of sin? How are we dazzled by its attractiveness and then blinded by its power to its consequences?

We all know that the more we are acquainted with sin, the less we know about it.

The world is too much with us,

Late and soon.

Getting and spending,

We lay waste our powers (poem *The World Is Too Much With Us*, William Wordsworth). When the poet Wordsworth wrote these words, he was not thinking of Ephesians particularly, but he certainly voiced a rule that applies whether we are talking about the believer or the unbeliever. We "walk in the course of the world" (Eph. 2:2).

What is worldliness?

To my generation, being brought up in a conservative Swedish home in the Midwest, it was easy to identify worldliness. Anyone who had a great deal more of this world's goods, who looked stylishly pampered, was worldly. I shall never forget the Christmas morning my mother threw a deck of cards into the stove. They were "Old Maid" cards. For my mother they symbolized gambling—and gambling was worldly.

Before I move on, I want to say that I don't think my mother was particularly wrong. I am not endorsing gambling or frivolously spending one's time. But there is more to worldliness than this.

New Testament writers tell us that we are to "love not the world, neither the things that are in the world" (1 John 2:15) and "the friendship of the world is enmity against God" (James 4:4).

This is the battlefield. Jesus seems to say we are to be in the world, but not of the world (see John 17:11-16). What did he mean by that?

Certainly the world of nature is not evil— God made it and said that it was good. Natural law is not evil. God made it also. What, then, is wrong about the world?

It must be that the world's nearness corrodes our spiritual sensitivity. It lets us see so much with our natural eyes that we are not tempted to look with spiritual vision. We understand so much with our human minds that the temptation is to believe that we can understand everything with our natural minds.

Or is it the aging of our temperament?

The course of the world—we hear the thunder of a thousand feet and cannot resist joining the parade. The urge to conform must rise from our basic insecurity. We do not trust our inner vision, so we live by the goals of others.

We live to keep up with the Joneses and the Joneses desperately try to keep with the expectations of those who are trying to keep up with them. It is a deadly cycle. It is the cycle of death.

Gary Moore told me of an experiment made by the French scientist Fabré. Some processionary caterpillars (so called because of their tendency to follow each other) were placed around the rim of a saucer. In the middle of the saucer were placed mulberry leaves, such as caterpillars love to eat. But the caterpillars were busy following each other, 'round and 'round the rim of the plate. Within sight of food, they starved to death.

Paul talks about this. The way of the world is a way of death whether it is the first century or the twenty-first.

We must live in this world, it is true, but we must not live as though it were the only one! Again and again we are reminded of Paul's other-worldliness. He had seen beyond the rim of time, both into the past and into the future and he was never the same. Whatever trials there may be in this world, they were not enough to keep him from his goal. Whatever glories there were in this world—and certainly Paul must have known moments of exquisite joy and fulfillment—they were not grand enough to make him want to remain in this world forever.

Francis Thompson, who wrote *The Hound of Heaven,* was once criticized by a contemporary who said that Thompson never really felt at home in this present world. The answer came back that while it might be true of Thompson, the shame was that too many people who call themselves Christian *do* feel at home in this world.

When we look at past Christian martyrs, we may think, "The church has finally found its place in the world, because not many are martyred for their faith today. The church has finally found its place in the world."

Could it be that the world has finally found its place in the church? It is possible.

9

Alien Air Power

"The Prince of the Power of the Air" (Eph. 2:2)—who or what is it? Are there men arriving in spaceships to invade our earth? Many think there are such creatures. Whether or not such beings exist, we know that there is a negative power—a field of power, if you will—that militates against our spiritual progress. It is a little like the principle of gravity. Gravity is no immediate problem as long as you are not trying to lift something. But when you try to move a large stone, the force of gravity is very real. In the same way, if you are not trying to live by spiritual laws, you do not feel the pressure of the power of evil. But when you make a serious attempt to pray, to fast, to study God's word, or to witness, you feel the resistance of something—or someone.

Paul calls this the Prince of the Power of the Air, the spirit that now works in the children of disobedience.

In our world, the devil is caricatured as having a red suit, a pointed tail, and horns like a young goat. If he were so attired, we could laugh him away and tell him that the masquerade party was in the next apartment.

But it is not that easy.

Disobedience is the door by which he enters, or perhaps he is the one who knocks on the door of disobedience, making us believe that it is the door of opportunity. At any rate, we disobey not only because of who we are, but because of who he is.

In the first chapter of Ephesians, Paul, in celebrating the power of Christ, says:

Far above all principality, and power, and might, and dominion, and every name that is named, not only in this world, but in that which is to come (Eph. 1:21).

Obviously there are powers all around us. Jesus gives us victory over them, but let us not imagine that we are free from conflict.

If disobedience (at every level) is all around us, there must be an author of it.

Not only must we wrestle against our humanity (our nature), but we also must wrestle against these powers. Later in this letter Paul gets specific:

Put on the whole armour of God, that ye may be able to stand against the wiles of the devil. For we wrestle not against flesh and blood, but against principalities, against powers, against the rulers of darkness of this world, against spiritual wickedness in high places (Eph. 6:11-12).

There would be no victory without a struggle. And without the power of God's spirit, there would be no victory. The gravity of the world drags us down and the power of the ultimate adversary shoots us down. Only in Christ do we triumph. More of that later.

10

The Battleground of Body and Mind

As Paul tracks the path of spiritual death, he does not lay all of the blame on the world around us, neither on the corrosive fellowship of unbelievers nor on the might of Satan and all his cohorts. He tells us of the enemy within— our own physical and intellectual nature. We are the battlefield.

Sometimes when an emotional flare-up has broken a relationship, we hear, "But that is just the way I am. I can't help being this way."

Of course that is the way they are. Who would dispute it? But it is tragic to remain that way when the spirit of God is available and willing to enter our lives.

Not only do we find some kind of relief from our rationalizations about ourselves, but we also look around us to rationalize the whole world's behavior. We may even be better than the people around us. After all, who would not like to compare his own virtues with another's vices. As they say, "In the world of the blind, the one-eyed man is king."

In Ephesus, as in much of the world today, believers were a minority. It seems always so.

The world around us is no excuse for the world within us. In our day of sociological stereotypes, it is easy to say, "Change the environment, and you will change the people."

Nature should teach us. A lily blooming in a muddy pool is as white as one in the florist's window.

A fish living in a world of salt water still needs to be salted before becoming tasty.

Lionel Arrington once wrote a song that reminded us that all the water in the world wasn't enough to sink us unless the water got inside the boat.

One of the words Paul uses carries more significance than we usually give it: "Among whom also we all had our conversation in times past . . ." (Eph. 2:3). Rightly understood, the word *conversation* means "citizenship." ("Life in association with others, in the everyday intercourse of society." *Interpreter's Bible,* 1953, Vol. 10; p. 641.) Citizenship was a cherished word to Paul. He was a Roman citizen, even when he was far from Rome or any Roman province. As such, he demanded and got the special recognition and privilege of the empire. Now he talks of his *former* citizenship in the world of iniquity. This has changed. He is now a citizen of the kingdom of heaven.

Later in this chapter he speaks of being "aliens to the commonwealth of Israel, and strangers to the covenants of promise, having no hope, and without God in the world" (Eph. 2:12).

It is impossible to carry two spiritual passports—you must both choose and be chosen.

Fortunately, God has already chosen, so now we must choose.

The Brain-Body War

Mark Twain said, "Man is the only animal that blushes . . . or needs to." All other animals can live correctly by obeying their animal instincts. Humans cannot.

It is impossible for an animal to change his nature, not that he needs to do so. "Can the leopard (change) his spots?" asks God in Jer. 13:23. The leopard fulfills his destiny by obeying the desires of his flesh, his physical nature—not so with humans.

If we were merely animals, we could do what comes "naturally," but when we do that, we act worse than animals. Who ever heard of a homosexual chimpanzee? Or a rebellious sheep? But humans? They defy description in the level to which they can descend.

Not only is this true physically, but mentally as well. If we let our appetite run away with itself, we can become terribly overweight or seriously ill. If we let our minds become undisciplined, anxiety and depression are the result.

The law of nature makes the animal kingdom harmonious: the law of nature (according to Paul) decrees that those who follow their basic, undisciplined desires become the "children of wrath" (Eph. 2:3)

Anyone can prove his three-fold nature. If you do not believe that you have a soul, try living as though you are only a body. Or, try living as though you do not have a body, and you will become ill—your ignored nature will cry out for attention. Soul, mind, and body— these three are the three sides of the human triangle—remove one side and the other two collapse.

This three-sided pattern shows up in three distinct ways in Paul's letter to the Ephesians: (1) Past-present-future; (2) Body-mind-soul; (3) God-ourselves-others.

At this point in Paul's letter, the secret, the mystery, and the hidden wisdom began to clear up. It is God's eternal purpose to bring all these different (and sometimes warring) elements together to create unity. Ah, yes, to create not only compatibility, but unity.

We might even insert a modern word—*synergy*. The law of synergy says that three things brought together become more than the sum of the parts—they create something new.

To illustrate: A pile of bricks is not a house; a hundred bags of mortar mix are not a house; a mason is not a house. But a mason takes the bricks and mortar and creates a house. The three elements must be brought together to create something that no one could do by itself.

As Paul contemplates this, he is overwhelmed with the miracle:

> But God, who is rich in mercy, for his great love wherewith he loved us, even when we were dead in sins, hath quickened us together with Christ, (by grace ye are saved;) and hath raised us up together, and made us sit together in heavenly places in Christ Jesus (Eph. 2:4-6).

The Magic Word

Together. In this one word we have both the promise and the problem. The promise is:

> That in the dispensation of the fulness of times he might gather *together* in one all things in Christ, both which are in heaven, and which are on earth (Eph. 1:10, KJV).

Remember Paul's vision? He apparently saw history from a perspective no one had seen before, in much the same way that the astronauts circling in space were able to see the planet earth as a whole for the first time. Paul saw not only the earth, but what was beyond the earth.

It is true that vision of eternal things had occurred before, but no one had been able to "get them together" to show how they related. In the same way that a cook takes apples from the orchard, chemicals from the pantry, and milk from the pasture and combines them with the chemistry of cooking to make a pie, Paul now brings together the apparently conflicting ideas in the world and explains them in terms of a divine purpose.

Vague as this sounds, it is the formula for the power that God promised to give us. The word *together* echoes through this letter again and again:

1. He quickened us *together*.
2. He raised us up *together*.
3. He made us to sit *together* in heavenly places.

Getting things together seems to be the hard part.

When we moved out of a downtown condominium to a home with a lot, I discovered that I needed the same equipment I needed when I first moved out west. I shopped for a lawn edger.

When I found a model I liked, I told the salesgirl, "I want this edger, but I know the floor model is not for sale. How much will I have to put together?"

"Just fasten the handle on," she said.

"How many tools will I need?"

"A screwdriver and pliers should do it."

I bought the machine, all neatly contained in a large brown cardboard box. When I got home, I tried putting it together. The thirty-minute job the salesgirl had promised me stretched into two hours. The "screwdriver and pliers" she suggested had multiplied until I had more than a dozen tools on the driveway. Finally, with a bleeding thumb, a perspiring forehead, and a highly-stressed disposition, I got it all together and began to edge my lawn. As I passed the now-empty carton, I read the message again: "Some assembly required."

That is always the problem, getting things together. It's a human problem. It is not difficult being an individual Christian, it's just difficult to get along with all the other people who are Christian.

It's not that we can't get *along*; we just have problems getting things *together*.

This fact was forcibly brought home to me as I listened to Will Hughes in Alabama last summer. He quoted the verse in Paul's letter to the Ephesians:

> . . . Grow up into him in all things, which is the head, even Christ: From whom the whole body fitly joined together and compacted by that which every joint supplieth, according to the effectual working in the measure of every part, maketh increase of the body unto the edifying of itself in love (Eph. 4:15-16).

Will then held out his arm and said, "Here is my elbow. It is a joint. There are two bones in the forearm and two in the upper arm. But where they come together is the elbow. That is a joint. Take them apart and you have no elbow. You have no joint.

"Paul says that the body is made strong, is able to grow because of what these joints do

. . . it is the togetherness that counts. It is the togetherness that brings the blessing."

Even though I was sitting in a steamy, hot tabernacle on that August afternoon, my mind leaped into the "alert" position.

Will had diagnosed the problem. We lack togetherness.

This is true; not only in our human relationships, but also in our use of Scripture and our understanding of history. We have many valid ideas, and even occasionally some valid theologies, but they don't fit with all the other things that we know. We have many Christian groups —sincere and energetic—but they can't get together. The world is full of people who are without doubt good people, but they can't relate to other people.

Since that moment of revelation came to me, I have been on a crusade to get together. It has been interesting.

On one occasion, I told the story of the elbow and said that "the joints are where the strength is."

A voice from the audience said, "And that's where the arthritis is, too."

Pick your battlefield. Men and women, women and women, men and men, Arab and Jew, liberals and conservatives, right brain and left brain, youth and age, intuition and logic; the list is endless. Adversaries all, but realities all.

Is there a way of harmony—no, better, *synergy?* Can our differences result in strength?

Can the place where we come together be a point of strength rather than of conflict and tension?

Paul believed that they can. Or, more correctly, Christ can bring together. And only he can.

Small wonder the phrase "in Christ" occurs ten times in this short letter of six chapters.

What is remarkable about this letter is that it is both the most *mystical* and the most *practical* book in the Bible. It holds hands with the centuries and holds hands with each of us. It sees beyond time, but tells us how to live in a world of time. It deals not only with sin as a falling short of God's eternal purpose, but it pinpoints individual sins such as lying, stealing, adultery, and fornication.

Buckminster Fuller said that he begins every serious thought by thinking of the universe. Most of us don't. We are problem-solvers. Well, if not problem-solvers, at least we are problem-recognizers. We put out fires. We deal with crises.

Much better we should consider the universe first. But we should not end our thoughts there. We need to deal with our personal relationships.

It has been said that some people are so "heavenly" that they are no "earthly" good. Of course, the opposite is also true. Some of us are so bound to the earth that we strive for heavenly goals by earthly methods.

How well Paul understood the realities of the

earth: shipwrecks, fastings, beatings, prisons, hunger, and conflict. Yet even in prison (where he wrote the letter to the Ephesians), Paul's vision of the heavenly kingdom gave meaning to even the most degrading experiences. Small wonder that he encourages us. Christ "hath raised us up together, and made us sit together in heavenly places in Christ Jesus" (Eph. 2:6).

Could we ask, "Is our 'sitting together' the reason that we are in heavenly places, or is it that our *being in heavenly* places makes possible our togetherness?"

The question is vital for our generation.

All over the world there are well-meaning and earnest people who are trying to heal the brokenness of humankind. "Let us reconcile the blacks and the whites, the Jew and the Arab, the have and the have-nots, the young and the old, the rich and the poor." The list of battlegrounds seems endless.

Is reconciliation possible?

So far it has not been possible by any human means. Paul lived in this world of conflict, but his vision and spiritual insight gave him the answer. In his letter to the Corinthians, he said:

> God was in Christ, reconciling the world
> unto himself, . . . [He] hath given to us
> the ministry of reconciliation (2 Cor.
> 5:19, 18).

Now in the Ephesian letter he emphasizes his "in Christ" theme. Time after time he sounds this note. Our harmony with the universe, our harmony with God's plan, and our harmony with the people around us depends upon our being "in Christ."

"But now in Christ Jesus ye who sometimes were far off are made nigh by the blood of Christ. For he is our peace, who hath made both one, and hath broken down the middle wall of partition between us; having abolished in his flesh the enmity, even the law of commandments contained in ordinances; for to make in himself of twain one new man, so making peace" (Eph. 2:13-16).

Is this possible?

Can races live in harmony? Can different cultures live in harmony? Can families? Can religious groups who worship the same God worship together? Can people who love God actually love each other?

It is human to say, "Let them come to me." It is natural to believe that if everyone were more like us in thought and behavior that we could have peace in the world.

A couple stood before the minister repeating the wedding vows. At the conclusion of their vows, the minister said, "And now I make you both 'one.'"

In a timid voice, the groom said, "Which one?"

A logical question. Does marriage mean that one person will dominate and rule? It shouldn't. A Christian marriage is one where both the woman and the man are "in Christ," and both submit to him. He makes them one.

It seems natural for us to wish that the other in a relationship (whether it is a spouse, or a race, or a culture) would either move over or move out so that we could have harmony.

Joe Minkler told me of a couple who had lived together for fifty years, but they had lived in constant conflict. One day the weary wife said, "Henry, we have been married for fifty years, but haven't had one happy year in all that time. We stayed together for the sake of the children and because we didn't believe in divorce. Now the children are gone and I think we ought to do something so that we don't spend our remaining years in conflict. Let's just kneel down and pray and ask God to take one of us home to heaven, and then I will go and live with my sister."

Here is another illustration of this principle of "Go-away-and-it-will-get-better": Two boys sat astride a horse. Under the load, the horse was plodding along wearily. One of the boys spoke, "I think one of us needs to get off so that I can ride better."

While these stories are humorous, they lose their humor when applied to nations who try to blast other nations off the face of the earth "so that I can ride better." In a marriage that is made intolerable by a bossy man, things do not improve when you develop a "bossy" wife. In a Christian marriage, it is never a question of who gets his way (or her way). We go God's way.

When we come to Christ, we come together. Without Christ, we are aliens.

Here the theme of Ephesians emerges clearly. We can claim the inheritance of the saints, when we are together with the saints. When we are out of the family, we are out of the fortune.

It is more than a play on words to say that the only ship that will transport us to heavenly places is "fellowship."

Paul makes it clear that this kind of unity is not achieved by our *understanding* each other, but by *accepting* each other.

Paul's life story is a story of relatedness. He was a cultured, literate Jew, a scholar and a mystic. But he had to relate to all the other kinds of people as well. In his letter to the Romans, he understands this obligation:

> I am debtor both to the Greeks, and to the Barbarians; both to the wise, and to the unwise. So, as much as in me is, I am ready to preach the gospel to you that are at Rome also (Rom. 1:14-15).

Most students of history conclude that the religious differences between people are more often sociological than theological. Vance Packard, in his book *The Status Seekers,* talks of the social differences that make walls between people so that—although they obviously worship the same God—they don't worship in the same ways. One chapter in Packard's book is entitled "From Pentecostalism to Episcopalianism."

Paul related to all kinds of people, but not because he was naturally charitable or understanding—look at him before he met Christ. It would be difficult to find a more provincial, rock-ribbed traditionalist than Saul of Tarsus. If God wanted his people to be "one," Saul knew *which* one. The world would have to come to his Judaistic way of thinking.

When Paul writes to the Ephesians that God has broken down the middle wall of partition between the Jew and the Gentile, he was not thinking of some poetic or mystical event. When the wall came down, Paul was hit on the head by many of the bricks.

How did Paul understand this breaking down of the wall between warring factions?

Only in Christ. Listen: "For through him [Christ] we both have access by one Spirit unto the Father" (Eph. 2:18).

This is a remarkable verse. Here the trinity of God is illustrated: Through Christ, the son, we (now together) both have access by *one* Spirit to the Father.

How can we put it more simply?

Jesus (being God) became man to prove that God could live in a human body. He made the two worlds one—the world of spirit and the world of flesh. Then he broke down the wall that separated the two and every other wall that separates people. For us to understand this mystery, the *Spirit* must open our eyes. The Holy Spirit opens the door into this unlimited fellowship. We are born of the Spirit. Now, having entered a new relationship with Christ and God the Father, we find ourselves in a new relationship with the family of God. The family has roots going back to the foundation of the world. It includes not only the apostles and prophets, but also the other believers around us.

Here the theme of togetherness shines through again. If we are together with Christ, we are together with each other. When we let ourselves get separated from each other, we forfeit our relationship with Christ and the eternal church.

The unity of believers is not something we achieve. It is a fact we cannot avoid.

If we do not understand this formula, the rest of the letter to the Ephesians will not make sense to us. In the final four chapters of his letter—which, of course, was not divided in Paul's original letter as it is today in our Bibles—Paul gets to the part of "togetherness" that we can do. It is tremendously practical. Buckminster Fuller told us to begin with the universal and move to the personal. Paul does.

12

Prison's Polished Jewel

If you, in reading Ephesians, feel overwhelmed by the profound mystical realities of the worlds around us as well as the world within us, let me urge you to read the last chapters of the book first. You will find something your size. In fact, it will appear so personal that you will wonder if Paul has been reading your mail, or at least your diary!

Once more we must look at Paul's opening sentence: "Paul, an apostle of Jesus Christ by the will of God. . . ." Two facts have been generally accepted. Paul is in prison—an abandoned well whose walls are as thick as the earth around it. He is in physical distress. Why? First, he is an apostle. The word *apostle* means "one who is sent." Like an arrow from a bow or a bullet from a gun, Paul has been hurled into this prison by God. Knowing that we would doubt that God would allow such a thing, he says, "by the will of God." If anyone is in the will of God, he is in the will of God whether he is in a prison or a penthouse.

Why would God allow Paul's imprisonment? I am sure Paul had asked this question many times, just as we do. But he thought about it long enough that he could see God's purpose in all things. Just as the hammer makes sparks when it strikes the flint and not the feathers, so illumination comes from the hard times of life, the painful encounters.

Faced with unyielding stone walls around him, Paul is forced to look to the skies, the vast expanse of the heavens. He is forced by the stern realities of the prison of Rome to look to the ultimate reality of the purpose of God.

The letter to the Ephesians is the high mark of Paul's writings. Written slowly, thoughtfully, it shines as a polished jewel.

His letter reflects the brilliance of his revelation.

Little wonder that the word *together* is so much a part of this letter. Paul has been able to bring together the mystical reality of the eternal church and the practical reality of the local observable church. He blends them into one picture, the true church. He blends the will of God and the willingness of man into one picture—reality.

If you shop vigorously in antique stores, you may find an old-fashioned stereoscope. Buy it. It will straighten out most theological problems.

Lest you think that a stereoscope is some new electronic import from Japan, let me hasten to tell you that it was one of the toys of my childhood. Obviously we had no television or any radio. We had played all the old phonograph records until they were too scratchy to be enjoyable. But we had the stereoscope, an optical device for looking at special postcards.

The stereoscope had two lenses. The postcard had two pictures, each taken from a slightly different angle. When the postcard was placed in the holder and properly focused, the two pictures blended into one, and presto! We had a three-dimensional effect.

We had pictures of battlefields in World War I where you could almost smell the gunpowder and hear the exploding shells. They were lifelike. Opposite views of the same scene, blended together. Of course, you could look at the pictures without the lenses, just with the naked eye. You could see the two pictures, but you could not grasp their relationship, not without the lens.

In Paul's theology, Christ is the lens through which we view the conflicting pictures of our world, our universe. Without Christ, they remain in conflict—then and now.

Law and grace.

Mercy and justice.

Sovereignty of God and free will of men.

Literal Israel and spiritual Israel.

Timelessness and the world of time.

God's foreknowledge and man's responsibility.

The permissive will of God and the perfect will of God.

The list could go on. Conflicts invade every thoughtful mind. But, and here is the sad part, the blindness of human wisdom keeps us from seeing both sides. We build walls around our concept of truth, our understanding of the church, and try to protect our ideas.

Edwin Markaham's lines, though intended to be personal, are also profoundly theological:

He drew a circle that shut me out,
 Heretic, rebel, a thing to flout . . .
 (*Outwitted*)

And so the lines are drawn. Black and white, East and West, liberal and conservative, evangelical and liturgical, male and female, young and old. Our circle of understanding becomes a wall around us. It not only keeps others from entering the fellowship of our life and thought, it also keeps us from entering theirs. Any search for truth beyond our circular wall is branded "heresy." Our very defense of truth keeps us from seeing the truth.

Paul himself is a good example of this provincialism. In refusing to accept God's people outside his circle of understanding, he shut himself off from God. In persecuting those who did not fit his theology, he was actually persecuting Christ. So the voice from heaven spoke to him, "I am Jesus, whom you are persecuting" (Acts 9:5, NIV).

No wonder Paul prayed for the eyes of the Ephesians to be opened. He knew what this eye-opening experience had done for him.

Edwin Markaham's poem is more than the first two lines . . . and it would be great if our life story would be more than the first two lines that shut people out. Here are Markaham's lines:

> But love and I had the wit to win.
> We drew a circle that took him in.
> (*Outwitted*)

In the Ephesian letter Paul is drawing such a circle.

As I mentioned earlier, it seems that Paul's letter to the Ephesians is an outgrowing of his vision in which he was lifted up to the third heaven. The perspective he got from this was so great that its explanation would not only have been impossible, it would have been unlawful. That is the reason Paul prays for the people that their eyes may be opened just as his had been (Eph. 1:18).

During the World War II, a young airman made his first flight over Europe. While in school he had studied a map of Europe, learning the boundaries and national differences. Now in the air, things looked different. His exact words to his family were: "When you get high enough, all the boundaries disappear."

Paul had reached such a height. And he urges us to aspire to it. In fact, he tells us how we can—together.

Here is the word and the concept. We need to bring together the telescopic and the microscopic—the far and the near—the universal church and the local fellowship.

Each without the other is an anachronism.

It has been well said that when we pray the Lord's prayer, we say, "Our Father." At that moment, we are either missionaries or we are hypocrites. We cannot claim the family without claiming the Father, and we cannot claim the Father without claiming the family. They go (would you believe it?) together.

A local pastor met a man who was an aggressive missionary. He traveled throughout the world trying to win people to Christ. "When you are home," asked the pastor, "where do you attend church?"

"Oh, I am a member of the invisible church of God."

"I see," said the pastor. "And are you able to pay your transportation and living costs with invisible dollars, given to you by invisible people?"

"Of course not. People want real money. And real people must give it."

"But if we are receiving from the body without giving to the body, are we not a parasite on the body? You believe in a visible church, but you do not want to be a part of it."

Any student of the New Testament knows that the principal heresy to attack the church was Gnosticism. Basically, the Gnostics believed that God was mystically revealed and Jesus could not possibly have been God because he had a physical body; he ate, slept, and got tired, just as all of us do. Many of Paul's letters, especially Galatians and Colossians, were written to combat this idea. Jesus was God in the flesh, in him dwelt the fullness of the Godhead bodily.

The independent missionary to whom I referred earlier was an evangelical Gnostic. Though he believed in Christ, he did not believe in his body, the church. He didn't feel he had to relate to it.

Paul speaks to this in the last four chapters of his letter.

One evening, purely by chance, I bumped into the world renowned concert pianist, Van Cliburn. We were eating at the same restaurant late one night, so I took the occasion to talk with him.

As we talked I noticed he was drinking milk from little half-pint cartons, nothing else. He had finished a concert, and in the course of our discussion of it, I asked, "And afterward you drink only milk?"

As he wiped his mouth and arose to leave he responded, "Yes, I take only milk afterward. It settled my stomach."

After he had gone, I stared at the little orange milk cartons. "Little cartons," I thought, "do you realize what has happened? And you, sixteen ounces of Foremost milk, do you know what has happened? You have moved out of the limited world to a wider world. Milk, yesterday you were in a cow. Today you are in Van Cliburn. Yesterday you were only part of

Betsy's mooing—tomorrow you will be a part of Van Cliburn's music. Yesterday in the green pasture, tomorrow in Carnegie Hall. A miracle. Your path has taken you from the udder of a cow to a cardboard prison, and now to the brain of a genius."

Does this make sense? To me it is not only sense, it is wisdom. It is a parable of the church.

When we leave our limited, labeled, theological prisons and become a part of the body of Christ, we experience a transition more dramatic than any carton of milk ever had. And now, we are part not only of the family of God around the world, but also of the whole family in heaven and earth. Our spiritual inheritance reaches back before the foundation of the world. God had a destiny for us, and now that we have accepted his calling, we are called into a whole new series of relationships.

While thinking of this, Paul's body is in a grim Roman prison, but his spirit has camp-meeting time with all the saints of all times. He explodes into a prayer of praise:

> For this cause I bow my knees unto the Father of our Lord Jesus Christ, of whom the whole family in heaven and earth is named, that . . . [you] may be able to comprehend with all saints what is the breadth, and length, and depth and height; and to know the love of Christ, which passeth knowledge, that

ye might be filled with all the fulness of God (Eph. 3:14-15, 18-19).

Then the doxology: "Unto him be glory in the church by Christ Jesus throughout all ages, world without end. Amen" (Eph. 3:21).

Many devout men and women have added great dimensions to our faith. In the Old Testament, we learn of the law of God through Moses, the love of God through Hosea, the universality of God through Isaiah, the nature of God through the Psalms, and judgments of God through Jeremiah and Ezekiel. Then, in New Testament times, we learn who God really is through Jesus Christ. But even after this earthly stay, we learn many things about God's plan through godly men and women.

Many have broadened, lengthened, deepened, and heightened our understanding of the Bible. The list is long: Augustine, Luther, Knox, Savonarola, John Wesley, D. S. Warner, Albert Schweitzer, and Kagawa. Even in our own time there are people who push back the borders of our ignorance.

If they are "in Christ," and I am in Christ, I claim them all. I do not need to be labeled by them. If a lantern shows me the path, I do not deify the lantern. I follow the path. I do not call myself a lantern because I have been blessed by it. I am simply a Christian walking in the light.

Our denominational walls are crumbling. We are, to the surprise of many, finding brothers and sisters who, until now, were huddling behind walls of doctrines. They realize that separating themselves from others who belong to God is wrong.

In a national church meeting, I spoke of the Spanish Church. My Spanish brother interrupted me. We have no Spanish church. We are a part of God's church and we are merely the Spanish-speaking part of it.

Wonderful. Language may be different, but it is no excuse for separation.

Return to my illustration about Van Cliburn's drinking a carton of milk. When the milk left its little cardboard container and entered the body of the musical genius, it became a part of his whole body. Within minutes it was in his bloodstream, nourishing not only his skillful fingers, but also his tibia and toenails.

What a joy to be free in fellowship. What new dimensions of understanding wait for us as we open our arms and our hearts to others?

13

Called to Be What?

Even more remarkable than God's inheritance for us is his intensive search for the missing heirs. It is as though a millionaire relative had left his entire estate to us and then included in his will that money should be provided to search for us, if it took the detectives to the ends of the earth. They should search until they found us. And even then, they should not rest until they had convinced us to do whatever is necessary to claim it.

Why is it so difficult to hear God's call? How will we recognize it? How do we know that we are included in it?

Good questions, all of them. Let me offer a story, as far as I know, a true one.

During the days of depression in America, in the early 1930s, jobs of any kind were difficult to get. When an ad appeared in a local paper, it was eagerly read by desperate job-seekers.

A lad just out of high school answered a want ad for a telegraph operator at the local train station. Since he knew Morse code, the dot and dash system of telegraphy, he was hopeful that he might get the job. Arriving at the depot, he found the waiting room filled with men each wanting—and needing—the job.

The lad sat down among them and waited. Then suddenly, for no apparent reason, he got up, walked confidently to the door with its frosted glass marked "Private," opened the door, and went in.

After about twenty minutes he came out and said to the other people, "I am sorry to tell you, but the job is filled. I was hired."

"Impossible," the job-seekers cried. "You are younger, less experienced than any of us. We didn't even have a chance to talk to the supervisor."

"While you were talking among yourselves, the stationmaster came to the frosted glass window and tapped out a message in Morse code—dots and dashes. The message said, 'Will whoever hears this please come in for an interview?' I heard the call."

The word *called* figures largely in Paul's theology. Each time he uses the word *church,* he is speaking of the "called." The word itself (*Eklesia*) comes from two Greek words, the prefix *Ek* and the verb "to call." Together they mean "the called-out people."

To the Ephesian Christians, it meant being called away from the garish pagan practices, the idolatry of their fellow citizens. It meant, more importantly, being called into relationship with other Christians—all other Christians. It meant being called into unity. It meant being called together. It still means that.

The called people are a responding people. They are also a responsible people.

It is not enough to be called; we must "walk worthy of the vocation wherewith ye are called" (Eph. 4:1). We are called into unity.

Whatever justifications we may offer for the divided state of Christians, we find nothing in the Scripture to justify it. We are called into unity. If we do not have it, we ought to at least realize that we ought to have it. "There is one body, one Spirit, even as ye are called in one hope of your calling; One Lord, one faith, one baptism, One God and Father of all, who is above all, and through all, and in you all" (Eph. 4:4-6).

How beautifully one Scripture explains another!

If we contend that there are many ways of looking at God and, therefore, there must be many groups contending for their approach, we have only to read one phrase from Paul's letter: "One God and Father of all, who is above all, and through all, and in you all' (Eph. 4:6); and then recall one phrase from Christ: "Other sheep I have which are not of this fold (John 10:16).

As I understand it, there are only three ways to look at God, to describe his work. Paul covers them all in his sentence. What are the historic concepts of God?

1. God who is *transcendent,* that is, *above* all. People who emphasize this aspect of God's character are usually called "deists." They believe that God is the first cause of all life, but he is pretty much removed from his creation. To such people, God is thought of as the "wholly other," the "oversoul," or the "end of being." In this role, God is powerful, majestic, and regal, but distant.

2. God who is *existential,* that is, *through* all. People who emphasize this phase of God's nature talk of God intersecting history. In flashes of inspiration or insight, God may come to us. He may, on occasion, work miracles among us, but they are pretty much at his discretion. This theology encourages reverence for God, but not intimacy with God.

3. God who is *imminent,* that is, *within* us. An extreme form of this is pantheism. Such a teaching says that God is all, and all is God. In this concept, everything shares the nature of God, the dandelion, the deer, and the devout believer. The "power is within us," according to Ephesians 3:20 and many other scriptures.

What, then, is the right idea of God?

Frankly, we cannot define the ways God works, we can only recognize the ones that we can expect from our study of the Scripture. Actually, all three aspects of the nature of God are true, but none is true without the other.

God is over us, through us, *and* in us. We would not search for God if we had not been found by God. What we know of God makes us want to know more of him. While he works in us and abides within us, there are times when he comes to us with special visitations of power and miracle.

God is too big to be contained in human words or human understanding. We should not be troubled because we have unanswered questions. We should, instead, be troubled if we have no questions.

How, then, can we know more of God?

The fourth chapter of Paul's letter to the Ephesians is explicit and direct. There are some things we must do to experience more of the God life within us. We are to "grow up into him in all things" (4:15).

To help us grow, God has not only called us, but has specifically called others to help us. The calling of God is not only to fellowship, but also to function. Among those called to special ministry are apostles, prophets, evangelists, pastors, and teachers. If some are called to be leaders, others are called to be followers. If some are called to be shepherds, others are called to be sheep. If some are called to be teachers, others are called to be taught.

We are not responsible to do every job. We are called to do worthily the job we are called by God to do. This obedience puts us in right relationship with God's universal plan. We ought to be careful about seeking the glamorous, public, and appreciated roles. If we strive

<u>for these, the only reward will be that temporary feeling of appreciation we receive here on earth.</u>

On the other hand, we should not let someone else push us into a calling to which God has not called us. I sat one day having breakfast with a successful rancher in western Kansas. He was, by all reports, the ideal layman. He was a devout Christian, an exemplary husband, and a faithful supporter of the pastor and the church.

"You know my biggest problem, Mr. Berquist? So many people try to put me on a guilt trip because I am not in the full-time professional ministry. I feel called to be a successful rancher."

"Stay on the ranch, friend. We have enough poor preachers and too few dedicated ranchers. You walk worthy of *your* vocation."

How clear this is in Paul's letter. We are not only to be a part of God's body, the church, but we are told to be the specific part that we are called to be. And we are called to be in the particular place we are called to be. Even more than this, we are called into meaningful relationship with others who have different characteristics and different callings.

It is where we come together that the trouble lies. It is also here where the strength lies.

In a recent pastors' conference I talked about the "elbow principle." It is the joining that provides strength. In our body, it is the place where two bones (totally different) come together. In the spiritual church, it is the place where people with different temperaments and natures come together. So I suggested to the pastors, if you want to have a revival in your church, simply go home and build relationships with your most difficult members. Take them out to dinner. Listen to them. Find out what has gone wrong. When you do this, you will get rid of some of the spiritual arthritis—pain in the joints.

After the meeting, a pastor came to me and said, "I wish I hadn't come today. Now I know what is wrong in my church. And I know what I must do. There is one woman who comes to church who I find impossible to work with. I just avoid her. But I feel bad about it. I am going home and try to work things out."

Wonderful. I hope that this woman responds favorably and a new relationship is established, but even if it isn't, something will happen to that pastor and that church. They will be filled with more of the fullness of Christ.

How We Related to Each Other

I like the saying, "Sure you can fly, but that coccoon has got to go." It is true of the caterpillar, but it is also true of us. We cannot become the new person created unto good works until we are willing to give up our wrong ways. True, we are not saved by our works. We are saved by grace. But we *are* saved unto good works. We are not saved by changing our behavior, but being saved will change our behavior. Or, to say it another way, God loves you just as you are, but he loves you too much to let you stay that way.

Knowing this, Paul gets specific. His theology may reach both the world before, this world, and the world to come; but he gets personal.

A country preacher of a generation ago said, "The devil will get your goat if he can, because he knows where you have it tied." While it is true that the devil likes to prey upon our weakness, the spirit of God points out our weakness so that we can be strong. He calls us from the worldly life to the life of holiness. God may indeed provide the "robe of righteousness," but we have to put it on. "Put on the new man, which after God is created in righteousness and true holiness" (Eph. 4:24).

Beautifully Paul brings together the negative and the positive sides. In order to put something on, we must take something off. We not only lay hold of some things, we must also lay aside some things—quit them.

The theme of Ephesians is relationships—relationship with God's eternal plan, relationship with God's chosen people, and relationship with our former self. The formula for getting along with people is simple:

1. Don't lie. You can't build a relationship on dishonesty.

2. Tell the truth.

3. Don't stay angry. "Let not the sun go

down on your wrath (Eph. 4:26)." If you have offended someone, ask forgiveness. If you are upset, discover the reason and deal with it.

4. Don't let the devil drive you from his people. God has called us to unity, to love, and to acceptance.

5. Don't steal. Be a contributor. Look for ways to contribute to the church. Don't be a parasite and a liability.

6. Talk about what is good. Build people up. Actually, the church is made up of people. If you are tearing them down, you are destroying the life of the body. Edify. Build up. Think of ways to make people feel appreciated. You can strengthen them. Do it.

7. Don't grieve the Holy Spirit. He has been sent to lead you into truth. When he can't, he feels bad. You frustrate him. When he gently reproves you, don't resent it. Know that he does it only because God loves you. When he directs you to service, obey him.

8. Be as forgiving of others as Christ has been to you. Unless you would be happy for God to parade your sins before the whole world, don't parade others' sins and weakness.

All of these things are in the fourth chapter of Ephesians. They seem trivial in the light of the universal gospel. Simply remember that while the sun shines brilliantly, the man who puts his hands over his eyes remains in darkness. Sin blinds. Sin binds. Sin separates.

To ignore these guidelines to holy living is

like being in favor of health, but refusing to kill germs or bacteria.

Sexual Purity in an Impure World

Getting things together is the theme of Ephesians. Like a main theme in a piece of music, it comes in many ways. As you listen, you say, "Ah, here's that theme again." In the mind of God, we are destined to receive an inheritance so great that all earthly pleasures pale in comparison. But, again, we are workers together with God. We cannot do anything by ourselves, but God will not do anything in spite of us. So we sound again the note of the "getting together of body and soul, the flesh and the spirit." Christ has come to make this relationship a harmonious one. Just as he brought together the law and grace, faith and work, justice and mercy, the world that was and the world that is, God brought harmony—unity.

Does it sound "unspiritual" or trivial for Paul to launch into a discussion of fornication and sexual sin? Actually, he couldn't very well avoid it—then and now. Then, as now, *eros* masqueraded as *agape*. In the name of religion, prostitution flourished. Even in the early church, repeated warnings had to be given. While they were celebrating their being a part of the body of Christ, they apparently were involved in immorality.

In his Corinthian letter, Paul tells the people that

> Know ye not that your bodies are the members of Christ? Shall I then take the members of Christ, and make them members of an harlot? God forbid. What? know ye not that he which is joined to an harlot is one body? for two, saith he, shall be one flesh (1 Cor. 6:15-16, KJV).

Just as we are joined to the eternal body of Christ by our obeying the call of God, so we can be joined to an evil body by responding to the call of the flesh.

It was common in the day of which Paul wrote to make religion such a mystical thing that every kind of evil could masquerade as worship. Drunkenness, sexual sin, and licentiousness could all be condoned as acceptable if done in the name of religion. Parents wished their daughters to become temple prostitutes much as eager mothers promote their daughters today to become reigning beauty queens.

Fornication—sexual intercourse between unmarried persons—flourished in Paul's day and in ours. But it was wrong. Since the body itself is holy, to offer it for unholy purposes is simply wrong: sin.

Sexual sin is just that: sin; it's wrong—not simply because it might result in unwanted pregnancy or disease, but because it takes a member of the body of Christ and joins it to a harlot. There are physical consequences to be sure, but Paul is not mentioning them here. He simply says that "no whoremonger nor covetous man, who is an idolator, hath any inheritance in the kingdom of Christ and of God" (Eph. 5:5).

A pastor friend of mine was talking to a prominent businessman about his "affair."

"I don't know what will happen to my business if I leave my wife and take up with my secretary. I am sure it will cost me a great deal," the straying husband said.

"I don't know about your business," replied the pastor, "but it will cost you heaven."

Sometimes we are lured by statistics and surveys to feel that we are abnormal if we remain pure. "Sixty-five percent of the high school students are sexually active," we are told by the surveys.

Does that make it right? Does that change the law of God? Does that take away the guilt or the emotional and spiritual consequences? If a thousand people jump off a cliff at one time, it may become the popular thing to do, but it does not repeal the law of gravity.

In his counsel to the Ephesians, Paul becomes even more specific. Not only are we to abstain from fornication, we are to keep away from fornicators and let our disapproval be obvious. "And have no fellowship with the unfruitful works of darkness, but rather reprove them. For it is a shame even to speak of those things which are done of them in secret" (Eph. 5:11-12).

A bone-chilling testimony of Ted Bundy, confessed murderer of at least twenty girls, reveals that he nourished his mind on pornography—sexually explicit pictures, stories of unnatural and perverted sex, *Playboy, Penthouse,* and worse. By fueling his untamed natural lust, the lives of at least twenty young women were taken. But what of those who do not commit murder, rape, or violence? What of those whose only crime is sexual sin? And what of those, even professed Christians, who encourage this kind of activity by lustful looks and monetary support?

Paul's warnings included filthy humor, I am sure. But were he writing today, he would be persecuted for suggesting that Christian women vicariously live in sin when they follow breathlessly the daily "soaps" that make wife- and husband-swapping seem as casual as trading recipes for pie crust.

If, as some surveys indicate, ninety-five percent of the American people believe in God and sixty-five percent belong to some kind of church, what would happen if we all boycotted the suggestive, ribald, evil-glamorizing books, movies, television programs, and songs? We would see a change immediately. Whether or not we would drive the smut merchants out of business, we would see a change in our relationships. We would see an immediate change in our homes, our mental health, and our spiritual well-being.

Jesus indicated that it was as wrong to have imaginary adultery or fornication as it was to have actual physical adultery.

For what other reason would a person immerse himself in a book, movie, or television program that glamorized sexual sin, if he were not enjoying the vicarious experience? Can we possible imagine that these things help us to have a closer relationship with Christ and his Church? Can we imagine that they revitalize our spiritual life?

In our save-the-whales society, is there a voice raised to save-our-sanity-and-our-sanctity?

A group of tourists were being taken into a coal mine. One of the ladies appeared wearing a white suit, white shoes, and a white hat. "You can't wear that to visit a coal mine," the guide told her.

"There's no rule against wearing white to go into a coal mine," she complained.

"No, I guess not. But there is considerable evidence that you will not be wearing a white suit when you come out of the coal mine."

> Pure religion and undefiled before God and the Father is this, To visit the fatherless and widows in their affliction, and to keep himself *unspotted* from the world (James 1:27).

Who is bold enough to declare this message? Have we, in the name of tolerance, refuse to think honestly about our "calling to holiness?" Holiness is highly intolerant.

14

Can a Christian Drink Alcohol?

At times I wonder if the only Bible verse some Christians know is "drink no longer water, but use a little wine for thy stomach's sake and thine often infirmities" (1 Tim. 5:23).

Obviously wine had, and may have, a use. But "using it for medicine" and being "used by it" are two different things. Paul puts it flatly, "Be not drunk with wine, wherein is excess, but be filled with the Spirit" (Eph. 5:18).

Is there a case for total abstinence? I believe there is. The major scriptures regarding wine in the Bible all indicate that it is treacherous, addictive, excess-encouraging, and a mocker.

Certainly drunkenness is condemned. Neither "thieves, nor covetous, nor drunkards, nor revilers, nor extortioners, shall inherit the kingdom of God" (1 Cor. 6:10).

That is plain. If we want to claim our inheritance, we can't be drunkards. So the question is, how much can you drink and not be a drunkard?

Obviously, no one ever became a drunkard by not drinking—by totally abstaining. That much is clear. Now, how much makes you cross over the line?

Legally, if the percentage of alcohol in your blood is ten percent or more, you are drunk. If there is the right percentage of alcohol on your breath, you are legally drunk. I believe the scriptural standard is more strict.

Alcohol, even in small amounts, goes directly into the bloodstream and to the brain. It literally "fills" the body. How? After you have a drink—moments after—it is impossible to find any place in your body that is not affected by that drink. You brain, your eyes, your respiration, your metabolism, and your coordination are all affected. Naturally you are not "dead" drunk, but you are a "living drunk." You may be functional, but you are not fully functional.

Moreover, you are an excessive drinker because the drink has a built-in "excess factor."

The Japanese have a proverb: "First the man takes a drink. Then the drink takes a drink. Then the drink takes the man."

What is the alternative to drink? Spiritual reinforcement. Our sense of adequacy, our attitude of calm, our assurance of strength come from the spirit within—the Holy Spirit. He is a part of our inheritance.

I boarded a plane in Orlando and thought that there was an error in my boarding pass. I went to the flight attendant with my problem and she said, "Oh, no. Not you. Everything is going wrong today."

"I'm sorry," I said. "I'll work it out."

I returned to my seat and remembered that I had with me a copy of the book I had written, *When Nothing Seems to Go Right*. She gratefully accepted it and asked me to autograph it. Later in the flight, she came to my seat and asked if I were writing any more books.

"Yes, I'm actually writing a book called *How Women Think*."

"Really?"

"Yes, I have fifteen chapter titles already. The first chapter is "Just Because I Have a Roast in the Oven Doesn't Mean We Can't Go Out for Dinner.""

"I'll buy that," she said.

I gave her a few more of my chapter titles and she went on with her work. Later she came to my seat again and said, "Mr. Berquist, I just thought of one more chapter for you book."

"Good. What is it?"

"I Need a Martini and I Don't Drink."

I can identify with that feeling. Sometimes the frustrations of life demand some relief. I am glad you don't drink. If you had no other source of help than alcohol or drugs, I could understand why you would reach for a "crutch." You don't need a crutch. You need the help that God can give you. And like alcohol, God's spirit can reach to every part of the body and can bring help. Better yet, there are not bad after-effects, no hangovers.

How grateful we should be for the gift of the spirit that not only does not rob us of our intelligence, but puts us in touch with infinite intelligence.

Men, Women, and God

Nowhere is the central theme of Paul's letter to the Ephesians more clearly visible than in the last part of the fifth chapter as he talks about marriage.

And nowhere have more strange and strained interpretations risen than in this chapter. "Wives, be subject to your husbands," shout the dominant males.

"What did Paul know about marriage?" shout their spouses. "Paul wasn't even married."

First let me say that it doesn't make any difference whether the Apostle was married or not. He is not speaking from his perspective or inspiration, but by the infinite perspective of God and the immediate inspiration of the Holy Spirit. Had God chosen to bring these words by writing in the sky, they would not be more authentic.

Second, I must say that in all probability, Paul was married. He was a member of the Sanhedrin, the high official body of the Hebrews, and to belong to it one had to be married. Moreover, the Hebrews didn't consider a man truly to be a man until he was married.

The respect that Paul received certainly indicated that he was respected.

Now, what did he say? Or rather, what did God say through the pen of Paul?

He did say, "Wives, submit yourselves unto your own husbands, as unto the Lord" (Eph. 5:22). However, in the preceding verse he said, "Submitting yourselves one to another in the fear of God" (v. 21).

Submission is a two-way street. But this does not mean that we abandon our uniqueness or our personality. A hammer is no less a hammer when it yields to the hand of the carpenter. A brush is no less a brush in the hand of the artist. In fact, it is most truly a hammer or a brush when it submits. The destiny of a hammer is to drive nails and it cannot do this until it submits. The destiny of a brush is to paint pictures, and it cannot until it submits.

Men and women have special destinies, unique and special, but they cannot perform them without submission.

The woman who says, "I just want to be myself" cannot truly be herself until she learns how to submit. And a man who thunders, "I just want to live my own life" will live an inferior life until he learns to submit.

Nowhere is the doctrine of the church more clearly illustrated than in Paul's discussion of marriage. In fact, in this fifth chapter of Ephesians, Paul so intertwines them that you have to stop and check yourself as you read. "Is he talking about Christ and the church or me and my wife?"

Paul answers the question. Having gone through some very direct commands for the married couple, he says: "This is a great mystery, but I speak concerning Christ and the church. Nevertheless let every one of you in particular so love his wife even as himself; and the wife see that she reverence her husband" (Eph. 5:32-33).

The more we minimize the difference between the sexes, the more we weaken both. For a woman to affirm her femininity means that she makes possible a stronger husband. For a man to affirm his basic masculinity means that his wife is a stronger person. The union of the two makes the togetherness principle of Ephesians workable and visible.

The body itself should teach us. An ankle bone bleaching in the desert is a toy for the dogs. Properly placed in the body, it not only helps the body to accomplish its goal, it fulfills itself. Togetherness does it. It does not sacrifice its identify by submitting to the other bones and to the will of the walker. It becomes what it was meant to be.

An individual Christian does not lose identity or worth by submitting to the other members of Christ's body. One becomes functional— worth something—fulfilled. Paul makes this clear in the fourth chapter of Ephesians.

Now it becomes clear that the church is both

a model for the family and the family a model for the church. Just as it would be unthinkable for the church to exist without a head, a headless body would be a corpse. The head functions not only as a convenient place to put your hat, but as the control tower for all bodily functions.

Of course a head without a body would also be useless. Paul said that Christ (the head of the church) loved the church *as* his own body. Why? Because it *was* his body. "No man ever yet hated his own flesh," Paul says, "but nourisheth and cherisheth it, even as the Lord the church" (Eph. 5:29).

The "togetherness principle" has interesting results. If a man loves his wife, Paul says, he loves himself. Why? Because they are together.

By the same rule, if he is demeaning to his wife, he destroys not only the relationship, but himself as well. In the same way, a woman who demeans her husband also destroys herself.

As I have opportunity to talk to both women's groups and men's groups, I say repeatedly: If you want your wife to be more of a woman, try being more of a man. If you want your husband to be more of a man, try being more of a woman. For both, if you want to be more of a person, check your relationships with others. We are members of one another.

In our day of mixed sexual signals, there is a feeling: "Anything you can do, I can do." Usually this implies, "Anything you can do, I can do

. . . better." Women don't really need men. Or men don't really need women. It's as though each were complete without the other.

A friend of mine recently told me of her precocious three-year-old grandchild. He had been told that an earthworm cut in two would still live. Both halves would survive. So, holding an earthworm in his hand, Steve said, "Little worm, are you lonely? I'll bet you are." So he cut the worm in two and said, "Now you have someone to play with."

Women would like to think that men should think like them, and men can't understand why women don't think like them.

Why don't they?

Simple. They are different. And it is in this ability to relate to different people that the relationships get strong.

It may be true that in some parts of the world and in some cultures the men have been bossy, selfish, and self-seeking. But the answer is not to replace them with bossy, selfish, and self-seeking women.

The goal is not competitiveness, but togetherness. We are members of each other.

Left to ourselves, we develop a program for uniformity, of making others like ourselves. God's program is unity through diversity and relatedness.

If we find it difficult to do what the Bible commands in terms of submission to each other, we should ask ourselves whether or not we have really submitted to Christ. It is not likely that anyone who has not been willing to submit to Christ would be willing to submit to another human or a group of humans.

It is interesting to see a generation of people who laugh off the authority of God's Word, or the commands of Christ. Are they free? Indeed not. They become slaves of their passion, their ambition, or their greed.

Only in submitting to Christ and to each other do we find the opportunity to fulfill our destiny.

Getting Along in the Home

It isn't important to be able to understand God's Word so that you can obey it. It is important to obey God's Word so that you can understand it. Jesus said, "If any man will do his will, he shall know of the doctrine, whether it be of God" (Jn. 7:17).

The same law applies to the family. It is not necessary to understand your parents; it is almost always necessary to obey them. In fact, the commandment "Honor thy father and mother" is the first commandment with promise. To my knowledge, there is no other promise of a long life but this one . . . honor thy father and mother.

If that were the only reward, it might be well worth it. But, of course, there is more. If we are out of fellowship with our family, it is hard to relate to other people.

In the world of Paul's day, many homes were filled with tension. In the market place, slavery was commonplace. There were no unions to protect the rights of the workers. Yet even in those grim times, Paul tells servants to obey their masters. If their reward was not forthcoming, they were told to be patient because God would reward them. "Whatsoever good thing any man doeth, the same shall he receive of the Lord, whether he be bond or free" (Eph. 6:8).

Masters were not exempt from responsibility. In Paul's day, a slaveowner had the power of life or death over his slaves. No one monitored him. No one could challenge him. But Paul said that he did have a master and he was accountable.

No relationship of life escapes the eye of God. We are all tied together.

the church, in the home or in the marriage. Moreover, they had to maintain that spiritual upreach that connected them to the power of God in Christ.

They could not do it alone. Nor can we. Jew and Gentile, men and women, bond and free: we are part of each other.

It is clear to Paul that we are involved in battle, in a war. "Not against flesh and blood," he says in chapter 6, verse 12, "but against the rulers, against the authorities, against the powers of this dark world and against the spiritual forces of evil in the heavenly realms" (NIV).

To survive this kind of fight means that we must have both an effective offense and an effective defense. Part of these God provides: "loins girt about with truth, and having on the breastplate of righteousness; and your feet shod with the preparation of the gospel of peace . . . and . . . the shield of faith . . . . the helmet of salvation" (Eph. 6:14-17). We simply accept them from God and put them on. For offense we have "the sword of the Spirit, which is the word of God," Paul tells us in verse 17. This is God's revealed truth.

If we try to live victoriously and win the battle with empty hands, we fail. Mere cunning will not do it. We will become one more set of dry bones left to bleach on the desert sands of failure.

For us, the word of God is in the Bible, revealed to us by the Holy Spirit. Just as Jesus used scripture to withstand Satan's power in his desert temptation, so we must make use of this essential weapon, provided by God. Human reasoning will not do it. Human arguments will not prevail. "It is written," says Jesus (Matt. 4:4). Only God's written word can effectively face the devil.

To be very practical, Christians should have a full quiver of arrows with which to face spiritual enemies. Or, to put it in modern, swashbuckling terms, Christians need a cartridge belt full of biblical bullets. "Equalizer" was the term used for the revolver in the old west. Short men became tall with a gun in hand, weak men strong. Spiritually, the Bible makes giants of us all. Midgets become tall in the saddle with God's word in hand.

Our warfare is spiritual. It is impossible to fight a spiritual war with material weapons, just as impossible as it is to fight a tornado with a flyswatter. Energy and a well meaning disposition won't cut it.

Is the battle intense? Of course. But when Paul sends the word, "Stand!" he also tells us how to do it (Eph. 6:13). No one can accuse Paul of underestimating the power of evil, neither the evil in our world or the world of evil itself. Paul's spiritual enemy was as real as the cold, stone prison walls that surrounded him. Evil was powerful, but note, not *all* powerful. We steadily gain the unspoken conviction that Christ is in charge.

And with this note, Paul closes the letter.

The late William E. Reed once told me of a soldier walking through a bombed out city in France at the end of World War II. In a cemetary the soldier spotted a statue of Christ. It was toppled over and some pessimistic survivor had chalked "His reign is over."

The soldier, a thoroughgoing Christian, took the time to hoist the statue to an upright position and shoulder it back onto its stone base. He read the chalked inscription again. He could not walk away with that message scrawled on that statue of his Jesus.

Finding a white stone, he scratched three more words.

"His reign is over . . . heaven and earth."

So Paul's message to Ephesus.

And in our day the shadow of St. Paul speaks again. He invites us to take on gladly the spiritual armour that God provides. Victory is sure. God invites us to share the triumph he has ordained for the Son of God and all who would enlist in his army.